What's Next for this Beginning Writer?

Mini-lessons that take writing from scribbles to script

JANINE REID & BETTY SCHULTZE

with

ULLA PETERSEN

Pembroke Publishers Limited

Dedicated to our daughters—Erin Reid, Kristine West-Sells, and Lana Schultze—at the beginning of their teaching careers

© 2005 Pembroke Publishers
538 Hood Road
Markham, Ontario, Canada L3R 3K9
www.pembrokepublishers.com

Distributed in the U.S. by Stenhouse Publishers
480 Congress Street
Portland, ME 04101-3400
www.stenhouse.com

Every effort has been made to contact copyright holders for permission to reproduce borrowed material. The publishers apologize for any such omissions and will be pleased to rectify them in subsequent reprints of the book.

We acknowledge the financial support of the Government of Canada through the Book Publishing Industry Development Program (BPIDP) for our publishing activities.

We acknowledge the support of the Government of Ontario through the Ontario Media Development Corporation Book Fund.

Thanks to Bruce Nguyen for permission to use his illustration on the cover of this book.

Library and Archives Canada Cataloguing in Publication

Reid, Janine, 1947-
   What's next for this beginning writer? : mini-lessons that take
writing from scribbles to script / Janine Reid and Betty Schultze ; with Ulla
Petersen.

Includes index.
ISBN 1-55138-187-7
   1. English language—Composition and exercises—Study and teaching
(Elementary) I. Schultze, Betty, 1947- II. Petersen, Ulla III. Title.

LB1528.R435 2005   372.62'3044   C2005-903310-X

Editor: Kate Revington
Cover Design: John Zehethofer
Typesetting: Jay Tee Graphics Ltd.

Printed and bound in Canada
9 8 7 6 5 4 3 2 1

Contents

Acknowledgments   *4*

Introduction: A Foundation for Writing Instruction   *5*

1. Making a Picture That Tells a Story   *31*
2. Telling a Story from a Picture   *34*
3. Finding Words and Letters Around the Room   *37*
4. Using Labels as a Writing Tool for Beginners   *40*
5. Writing at the Bottom of the Page   *45*
6. Reinforcing the Learning: Making Stories from Pictures   *46*
7. Telling a Story with Kidwriting   *51*
8. Putting More Detail in Pictures   *54*
9. Putting More Detail in Writing   *57*
10. Reinforcing the Learning: Writing Stories   *60*
11. Writing from Your Life   *64*
12. Starting with a Title   *67*
13. Making All the Sentences Belong   *70*
14. Remembering Details   *73*
15. Adding Direct Speech   *76*
16. Expressing Your Feelings   *79*
17. Reinforcing the Learning: Writing Personal Stories   *83*
18. Introducing Story Grammar   *89*
19. Using Story Grammar to Build a Story   *92*
20. Shaping a Story into a Poem   *95*
21. Writing Non-Fiction   *100*
22. Reinforcing the Learning: Reviewing Genres   *104*

Appendices   *110*

 i kn rit brochure   *111*
 Tips for Teaching ESL Learners About Writing   *113*
 Story Grammar Map   *114*
 Retelling a Story   *115*
 Story Grammar   *116*
 Our Favorite Books for Children   *117*

References   *119*

Index   *121*

Acknowledgments

We owe a debt of gratitude to all the young writers who gave us permission to use their work. Their samples make the book come to life and their voices speak clearly from the pages as they show us what is possible. We also express our thanks to the following teachers who have supplied samples of children's writing: Tara Major, Leona Huggins, Benita Bahd, and Lisa Sahli-Graham.

Thanks also to Eileen Harrison, for always having just the right story ready, as well as Carrie Sleep, Tara Major, and Leona Huggins, for reading the draft document and giving us their insight and advice. We also wish to thank Joy Nucich who brought her passion for children's writing to Maquinna Annex School in Vancouver. It was Joy's belief in the child as a writer that captured our imaginations and sparked our inquiry into writing with young children.

In further acknowledgment we thank those writers whose work has informed our practice and shaped our thinking: Lucy McCormick Calkins, Regie Routman, Donald Graves and Marilyn Chapman. They have given us insight into the potential of young writers when their teachers work alongside.

Introduction: A Foundation for Writing Instruction

Our work with young writers led us to share our understandings as mentors with some of the more than 700 teachers in The Early Literacy Project in Vancouver. Our mentoring took us into classrooms to observe, consult, and conduct demonstration lessons for writers. We met with teachers for team meetings at the school, professional development workshops, and mass assessments of writing across the school district. We came to understand that many teachers are unsatisfied with their current practices, but don't know how to make successful changes. Over and over, we heard teachers express the same questions and concerns. They want to know the answers to these key questions:

1. On what beliefs should I base my teaching of writing?
2. When should I start teaching writing?
3. Is scribing for students a good idea?
4. Doesn't reading come first?
5. Where do I find time for Writing Workshop?
6. How do I encourage students to write?
7. How do I help young writers improve?
8. What should I do beyond Writing Workshop?
9. How should I deal with spelling?
10. What's next for this beginning writer?

Addressing those questions with practical, step-by-step instructions for working with young writers is the focus of this book. In this introduction, we respond to the first nine questions with concrete suggestions for creating the tone and teaching in Writing Workshop; the balance of the text, Chapters 1 to 22, address the tenth question through craft lessons.

In each craft lesson for Writing Workshop, we present a sample on a continuum of writing development. We analyze each sample and describe what the child knows. We offer language to affirm the child's efforts and make suggestions for moving the child to the next step of writing development in a one-to-one conference. Since a number of students in a class typically present similar characteristics and needs as learners at the same time, the page after each chapter-opening student sample outlines a whole-class or small-group lesson in step-by-step detail. These group lessons provide the language, the examples and the concepts of writing to all children despite their developmental differences. They may need reteaching and review as well as reinforcement in at-the-elbow sessions during Writing Workshop.

What's Next for This Beginning Writer? is based on the belief that all children are writers. In our view, the teacher works actively alongside the child to move the writing to higher levels of competency. This book shows the teacher what to notice about a child's writing and how to meet each child at an appropriate developmental level and provide the nudge towards the next level. It provides insight into the creation of a supportive Writing Workshop, knowledge of the developmental stages of young writers, and recommendations for moving the writing towards greater competency, making teachers of Kindergarten and Grade 1 students well equipped to teach writing. *What's Next for This Beginning Writer?* will be pebbles in the moonlight as you find your way with writing instruction.

1. On what beliefs should I base my teaching of writing?

Let us explore this question by looking at three fictional teachers who represent different positions on a continuum regarding the right way to teach writing. Their beliefs, all of which might be found in the same school, are reflected in the student samples from their classes and in their comments about writing.

Grade 1, November: The whole class has copied this writing from the board. The first teacher, Glenda, reports, "I develop the story with the students on the chalkboard and then they copy it correctly. They are not ready to come up with their own ideas for stories and I don't agree with invented spelling. We have a spelling list that students take home on Monday and spell for a test on Friday. Many children get the words right on the tests, but they don't apply them correctly in writing so I don't let them write. The parents have a fit if the work is not corrected and I feel uncomfortable with invented spelling, so when they do write, I correct all the spelling errors. We spend 30 minutes each day on phonics worksheets, but their phonics skills are still very weak. These students are not ready to write—they're still struggling with the reading!"

Grade 1, November: Leah wrote the story at the top of the next page on her own. The second teacher, Tara, says, "It is essential to support the child in her belief in herself as a writer. For this reason, I encourage the students to see story events in their lives. I encourage the students to express their thoughts and creativity fearlessly, inventing the words they can say and not restricting their writing to words they can spell. I know that invented spelling lasts for just a short time. It is my role to assess what the child knows, what his opinion of himself as a writer is, and to decide what and when to teach. I believe my role is to advance the child's ability to write with explicit teaching in whole-class sessions, small groups, and one-to-one

Last night and the night before I had to wear thick pajamas. I said to my mother, "I don't think these pajamas are quite right. I think these pajamas are too hot and I am used to my other pajamas anyways."

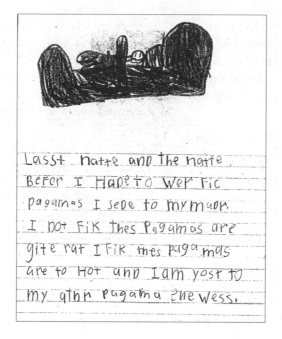

conferences. I teach phonic skills and spelling too, and I ask students to apply those lessons in authentic writing tasks. When children have to deconstruct the language into discrete sounds and represent those sounds with letters, that, to me, is phonics in action! Their writing gives me a window into their reading ability, too. If I see what they can write, then I know a lot about what they can read. I get a few questions from parents, but when I explain the stages of writing development to them and they see their child's progress, they are always supportive. "

There is a bus coming. There are cars. There is a big car. The bus is big. They are way up. They stopped. The cars.

Grade 1, November: Josh wrote this story on his own. The third teacher, Jean, says, "We must accept what the child can do. We must trust that children will develop in their own way and in their own time. They need this time to experiment with writing. They are immersed in a print-rich environment with lots of literacy experiences to enjoy. I do not do any explicit teaching of skills for writing. I prefer to fill the room with correct models of writing and to let the children learn in the context of literacy rich experiences. We must trust that they will learn and apply the skills as they are developmentally ready."

From these teachers' comments, we note the following assumptions:

Assumptions About Writing Instruction		
Glenda	**Tara**	**Jean**
Writing is the end product of a collection of discrete skills.	Writing is learned in the act of writing with the support of a knowledgeable teacher.	Writing is learned in a rich environment as the child is developmentally ready.
It is the teacher's role to ensure that students know how to write with correct conventions before they begin to write.	It is the teacher's role to accept the child's approximations and to instruct the child ever forward to correctness.	It is the teacher's role to accept the child's approximations and to trust that they will develop over time.
Children must learn to read before they can write.	Reading and writing are complementary activities and begin at the same time.	Children will read when they are ready. Usually they do not really learn to read until Grade 2.
The teacher must control the writing and the writer.	Through demonstration and guided practice, the teacher leads the child to control over writing strategies.	The child controls all aspects of the writing.
Parents will not understand the developmental nature of children's writing.	Informed parents are supportive of the developmental process.	Parents need to be patient. Children will learn!

The chart represents widely divergent perspectives on writing instruction.

Educators who think like Glenda believe that instruction comes first. In this view, the child's approximations of writing are chaotic and make the teacher anxious. Glenda doubts that children can learn in this way and she doubts her ability to teach her way out of disorder. When she structures the lesson so children's writing is conventionally accurate, she feels successful.

Jean, in contrast, represents the belief that children do not need explicit instruction. In Jean's view, if children are immersed in a literacy-rich environment with an encouraging teacher, the writing will develop as children mature. Jean sees that her role is to establish the environment, nurture, wait, and watch.

Tara's perspective matches our own. Our understanding is shaped by years of teaching in primary and intermediate classrooms, meeting beginning writers at many grade levels, reading, reflecting, and redefining our writing practices over decades.

We believe that writing is learned in the act of writing with the support of a knowledgeable teacher. We believe that the right teaching makes a difference. Although children do need a rich literacy environment and a writing climate that nurtures risk taking, they also need instruction. The teacher's art is to recognize what the child can do, to understand what the next learning step would be, and to provide appropriate instruction. Effective writing teachers work alongside the child in the Learning Zone, providing just the right amount of instruction at just the right time—not too much or the writer will be overwhelmed, not too little or the writer will not progress.

As Frank Smith put it in *Writing and the Writer*, "Writing is learned by writing, by reading and by perceiving oneself as a writer. None of this can be taught. But also none of this implies that there is no role for a teacher. Teachers must play a central part if children are to become writers, ensuring that they are exposed to stimulating demonstrations and helping and encouraging them to read and write" (199).

2. When should I start teaching writing?

> For the purposes of this book, any graphic representation that conveys meaning is writing, whether it is a picture that the child can describe or scribbles on the page that the child translates into a story. When a child scribbles and then holds up his masterpiece, telling us what it "says," this child is writing.

Teaching writing starts during the first days that students attend Kindergarten. It begins quickly and naturally as children engage in school activities. Start teaching where the writer is, building on the strengths the child displays. Make your teaching more conscious and planned, and invite the writer along on the path from scribble to picture-making, from picture-making to sound–letter matching, and onward to detailed expression in varied genres. As teachers, we open children up to stories and possibilities; then, working alongside, teaching lightly but consistently, sensing the "write" time with the right child, we show the next step to each writer. We find a delicate balance in which the child learns from our teaching, but also acquires new understandings from the fertile conditions of a supportive environment. It is important to acknowledge the child as someone trying to convey meaning through drawings, scribbles, or symbols.

Each product of student writing presents an opportunity to reinforce the child's belief in himself as a writer.

3. Is scribing for students a good idea?

No, even in the early stages, teachers do not need to scribe for children. Children themselves must do the hard work and have control over their writing. As children progress, we suggest and demonstrate ways they might improve their writing, but we ensure that they do the work. Years ago at a conference, a renowned educator, Donna Gordon, declared, "The person doing the work is the person doing the learning!" Teachers are wise to keep her words in mind when tempted to do too much for their students. The hard work of writing belongs to them.

> When students can recognize a word and read it without hesitating, it leads to *reading* fluency; when students can write a word without hesitating, it leads to *writing* fluency.

4. Doesn't reading come first?

Reading and writing work in tandem—don't wait until children can read before letting them write. Writing unlocks the mysteries of reading, so you can double the impact of your reading instruction by having children write daily. S-s-s-singing, p-p-p-popping, h-h-h-huffing through the sounds of language and matching those sounds with letters is reading deconstructed. When students read back their writing as they go and read aloud their stories to the teacher and friends each day, they build reading and writing skills simultaneously. Your students will realize greater gains in both reading and writing if they have chances to write!

5. How do I find time for Writing Workshop?

Finding the time becomes easier when you establish clear priorities, and Writing Workshop should be top priority. We recommend holding Writing Workshop daily, taking a minimum of 30 minutes at the beginning of Kindergarten to an hour for students in the last part of Grade 1. If given many opportunities to write, Kindergarten students can grow to sustain interest in writing for up to 45 minutes. Writing Workshop may include a mini-lesson and a warm-up story, rehearsal with a picture and partner talk, time to develop the story, and an opportunity to share it with a classmate. The lesson usually begins with students sitting on the carpet while the teacher models, and continues with students going to their seats to write independently. Just as the more students read, the better they read, the more students write, the better they write.

What is difficult is deciding what to let go of in order to make room for writing. When teachers look at the curriculum and prescribed learning outcomes, we may feel overwhelmed and wonder where we can fit it all in; however, daily opportunities to write are more important than almost anything else—more important than computers, more important than extended calendar time, more important than every phonics worksheet. So we look for ways to integrate curriculum using Social Studies and Science topics in our Language Arts block, and we look for field trips and experiences that teach multiple outcomes in a short time. Since the skills children learn from becoming competent writers will carry them with greater mastery across all curriculum areas, writing gets top priority.

Investing Time in Writing Workshop

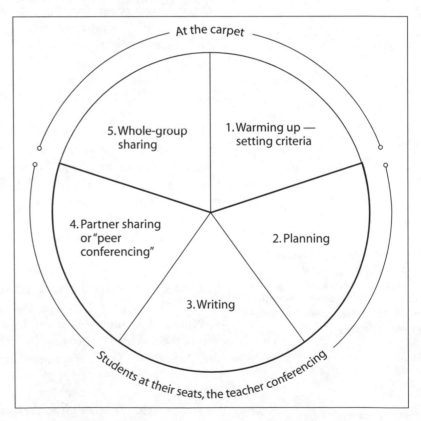

Schedule a minimum of 30 minutes, a maximum of 60 minutes.

Sample Day Plan for a Grade 1 Class

8:40–9:20	Morning Circle, Attendance, Calendar, Sharing of News, Shared Reading
9:20–10:00	Writing Workshop
10:00–10:30	Reading/Themes/Literature
10:30–10:50	*Recess*
10:50–11:40	Math
11:40–12:05	Spelling Dictation/Story/Songs
12:05–12:55	*Lunch*
12:55–1:05	Music Listening
1:05–2:00	Read-aloud/Independent Reading/Guided Reading/Conferences
2:00–3:00	Centres/Art/Science/Social Studies

6. How do I encourage students to write?

Celebrate success! Children will thrive as writers if they experience success. It is important to look at the products of children's writing and ask, "What is the child doing right? What can I say to honor this child's efforts at communicating meaning?"

When we acknowledge children publicly, we affirm their belief in themselves as writers. One way of doing this is to take a few minutes at the beginning of Writing Workshop to read and discuss the positive aspects of a few children's writing. As we acknowledge what each child has done right, we label the learning, reminding students of the strategies inherent in writing successfully and encouraging others to apply them in their own writing.

When we ask young writers to reach a little further, we teach lightly and close to what they are able to do. That helps maintain the spirit of success and confidence that students need, and cultivates joy in writing.

Watch for breakthroughs.
- Notice how Jamie's writing has stretched out a time in his life to make a more interesting story!
- Look how many sounds Lea has matched in her writing!
- Justin is such a fearless speller. He has used powerful words like "nasty" and "devoured." Good thinking, Justin!
- See how Harold is looking carefully at the action in the story when he says, "My dog went leaping through the tall grass looking for the stick."

Watch for gems like these and use them as teachable moments. When we capitalize on these opportunities and let the children's writing lead our teaching, we keep our instruction close to what the children are able to do. Observe what the children are doing, look for models to emulate, and take your teaching directions from breakthroughs in the writing. Their "firsts" and "personal bests" will show you what to teach next.

When the students in a Grade 1 Vancouver classroom were given a survey and asked what they enjoyed most about school, they chose writing over centres, gym, and even recess!

Some teachers have success with Author's Chair, where children read their writing and experience the delight of an appreciative audience. At these beginning stages, though, we find it is easier to hold the attention of a whole class when the teacher reads student writing aloud fluently and expressively. Try having children read aloud to a partner or a group of four, where lack of fluency has less impact.

When a student who has been making only random letters on a page suddenly makes several phonetic matches, putting a *p* beside a pumpkin, a *b* beside a boy, an *s* beside a sun, this is a "first" for that child and needs to be celebrated. Celebrate a student who, for days, has been drawing the same picture of a house, a tree, and a boy outside, but suddenly makes a much more detailed drawing of a birthday cake on a table, with people smiling and gifts on the floor. This picture is a breakthrough because the child has found a personal story with meaning and added details that tell about that moment. Similarly, when a student who has been reluctant to write more than a few words suddenly finds something important to say and writes six lines of print, acknowledge the "personal best" to help ensure that the student does the same thing tomorrow.

Acknowledge effort. Other ways we can demonstrate that children are successful writers include these:

- Shake a child's hand and say, "You are a writer!"
- Give a thumbs up.
- Show by your body language and curiosity how interested you are in the content of a child's work.

Keep students safe. Learning to write involves working in the Learning Zone, a term coined by Vygotsky. When the students venture into this zone, they experience disequalibria and some level of uncertainty and anxiety. The teacher's art is to create that climate of safety and security where young writers will take risks

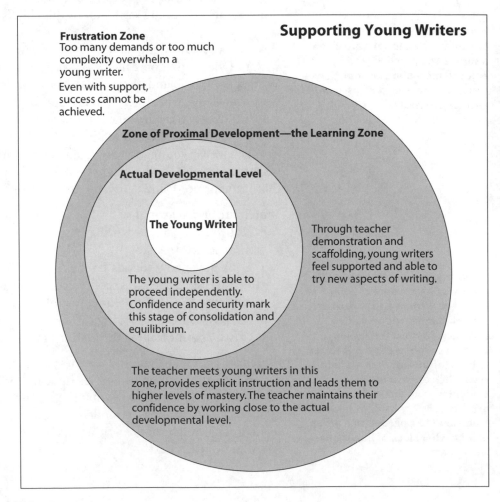

despite their uncertainty. In *Weaving Webs of Meaning*, Marilyn Chapman explains why risk taking is important: "When writers are taking risks in their learning, they will be working in their zones of proximal development, and this means they may make errors. No errors means staying with what is known and safe, what one can already do, so errors are often signs of growth" (175).

Teachers need to provide a classroom environment where children can experiment without fear of being "wrong." We have all seen the child who writes very little because of anxiety over performance or who writes a stilted sentence of mostly copied words or known sight words. Sometimes this anxiety stems from home, where parents may not understand the importance of invented spellings in the development of children's writing skills. These children dislike taking risks and want to write perfect sentences only. Often they engage in writing avoidance, which can take many disguises, such as these:

- spending too much time developing the picture
- erasing repeatedly to get the letters "just right"
- consulting spelling aids in the classroom
- dropping or sharpening the pencil
- going to the bathroom

Of course, each of these behaviors can be legitimate, but the sensitive teacher will move in and help the reluctant writer to start and sustain the writing.

In Writing Workshop, keeping the procedures simple and predictable helps students feel safe. Here are some of the simple procedures that can make Writing Workshop predictable:

- Have Writing Workshop at the same time each day.
- Start the lesson by reading examples of writing from the day before, commenting on each one and giving positive feedback.
- Teach a mini-lesson to the whole class—you thereby provide a goal, such as writing a longer story. This goal is relevant to all students whether they can write one more page or one more sentence.
- Set expectations and general goals for the day's writing.
- At times, let children work in partners to orally rehearse what they will write about.
- Provide at least 30 minutes of writing time while you hold individual and group conferences, reminding students of the day's goal and how to reach it, for example, by asking questions about the writing.
- Assess the writing to determine what the next steps will be for tomorrow's lesson.

A sense of safety is nurtured when the teacher conferences with children respectfully, acknowledging the good work they have done. It is further nurtured when the teaching is done lightly, allowing the child time to consolidate understandings before facing new challenges. Too much teaching too soon makes the writing task seem unnecessarily complex and undoable for young writers. As we demonstrate in this book, when teachers aim their teaching close to the child's independent level, the child is hardly aware of moving forward. The next step in writing is always a baby step.

Give students support in topic choice. As evidenced in our experiences with the Early Literacy Project in Vancouver, young writers enjoy developing their own story topics. When we assigned topics for writing assessment tasks, teachers across the district reported how difficult it was to get young writers to write on them. Even after warm-up and examples, young writers went ahead and developed their own stories. Bravo!

It is the child's responsibility to think of something to write about, but *not* without support. We can help young writers decide what to write by modeling how to view small occurrences as storied events. In this way we awaken students to the possibilities for stories in their lives. We can also talk with a child who is stuck for a topic, saying, "Having trouble getting started? Let's discuss it together." Some teachers post lists of writing ideas that students can turn to when stuck; however, we discourage teachers from providing sentence starters, prompts, and topics as a steady diet. When teachers ask students to call out their topics before beginning to write, this provides inspiration for classmates. Teachers can also recommend topics for writing: "I enjoyed hearing your story. Is that something you might like to write about? I think it would make a great topic for writing." We can also ensure that our teaching and curriculum choices, the contents of our room, and the sites of our field trips are rich and vital, providing stimuli for the imagination and events that are worthy of recording in Writing Workshop.

Effective writing teachers are always alert to the potential for writing topics in the stories children tell and encourage the class to look for similar stories. They share examples of stories from their own lives, highlight writing ideas from the students in the class and help to waken the children to the story potential around them. Chapter 11, Writing from Your Life, will show you how to develop banks of story ideas with students.

The following incident illustrates how Ulla helped a child see a story event in his life:

Shiv approached Ulla to tell her about pets his parent had. She listened thoughtfully and asked, "Is this something you would like to write about? It would make a great story." Shiv's story appears below:

THE STORY OF MY MOM AND DAD'S DOGS

One day when we were driving along my dad said his dog was dead. I said, "How?" My dad said, "He ate poison." I said, "Oh that's sad!"

"Yes," said my dad. Then my mom told me a story of her dog. She said her dog got hit by someone. I said, "That's sad too!"

"Yes," said my mom and dad together at the same time. I said, "I wish I had a dog."

Seeing this as a gem, Ulla read the story aloud to the class and encouraged the children to ask their parents, like Shiv has done, for stories from their lives. In the example below, you can see how Shiv's story prompted Kaitlin to follow his lead.

A STORY

My mom told me a story. The story was about her dog. When she had her dog and when she went to the park to play the dog would sit beside her. When someone was near her, the dog would bark and growl but never bite at all! But when she was about 13 the dog died. But she thought about the dog more than work. But I wish I had a dog too!

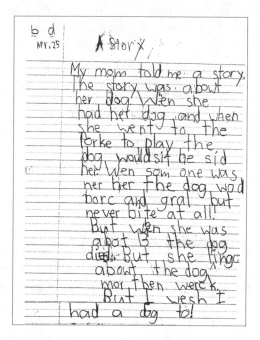

The writing from classmates makes the most powerful models. Use them to light the way to the next level of expressiveness and competency and watch your young writers follow enthusiastically!

Warm up with good stories read aloud. Thrilling stories of all kinds are great motivators for reading and writing. Teachers draw children's attention to the beauty of rich language, aspects of writing craft, and the variety of topics for writing. Through stories read aloud, children can learn that authors look for topics, choose their words carefully, and try to write a story that will please both themselves and others.

We can engage children in discussions of the writing craft with comments such as these:

- *"Fee fi fo fum!"* This language really makes the story come to life!
- "The spider pranced on delicate feet." The words "delicate" and "pranced" would make great additions to our list of powerful words.
- The way the author describes his feelings when his pet died really makes me understand just how sad he was. He has told us all about it.
- This author has really zoomed in with her magnifying glass to tell us all about her trip to the farm. I can really imagine what it was like for her.

Making aspects of writing craft explicit for children helps them to see how the skills they are learning are applied in the stories of others.

Let students draw before they write. As they draw and include details in their pictures, children think about what they will write about their pictures. The picture is also a springboard for teacher–student interactions that can lead the children to include more information in their stories. We encourage young children to draw and tell their stories, and make some letters they know. Later, as the writing begins to exceed children's ability to draw, they will ask to stop drawing before they write. They are now ready to rehearse orally with a partner before writing.

Have students rehearse orally with a partner. Oral rehearsal can be a great tool for rehearsing the writing. Teach your students to sit eye to eye, knee to knee, sharing their ideas and giving feedback on ideas they hear. Some teachers report that their less mature writers need time to draw for a few minutes before meeting a partner for oral rehearsal. When they are given drawing time first, they can talk to a partner about their picture.

As writers mature and their oral language develops, much of the pre-writing warm-up will be done with partner talk. For example, during a lesson on including detail, the teacher may say: "Consider things you could include in the story. Use your fingers and touch each finger as you tell a detail of your experience." When children have a chance to say the words out loud, all students hear ideas from their partners and teachers can identify those children who need help. When the teacher restricts responses to teacher-to-student dialogue, most students do not have an opportunity to practise their oral language and rehearse ideas aloud. This oral rehearsal increases student engagement in the classroom.

Partner talk can also be used to promote writing at greater length. The teacher may encourage students to retell a story read aloud. Stopping frequently at intervals throughout the story, the teacher prompts student pairs to tell each other what has occurred: "Blue partner, tell yellow partner what happened in this part of the story. Do it like this: Little Red Riding Hood bent over to pick the flowers and . . ." This supported oral rehearsal gives students opportunity to build fluency without having to consider the story plot. Such focused conversations support children's learning and their ability to write.

7. How do I help writers improve?

Know your writers. As the year passes, teachers learn about their young writers through countless interactions and thoughtful observations. They also come to learn the developmental sequence and understand the incremental steps in writing development. They are able to assess where each child is and where the child needs to go. With experience, these knowledge bases come together as the teacher meets the child over a new piece of work. Assessing the needs of the writer before her the writing teacher asks herself: *Do I just celebrate?* Or, *do I celebrate and teach?*

Over time and with thoughtful observation of children, timing for instruction becomes instinctive. Until that time, teachers may use the outline on the next page to help determine if this is the moment for asking the child to reach further.

For teachers' reference we also include a table that describes a developmental continuum for beginning writers from scribble to competency across five dimensions of writing (see pages 18–19). This table represents our attempt to show how skills may emerge over time in these dimensions:

- picture
- oral language that precedes writing
- hearing and recording sounds and spelling
- printing and punctuation
- writing development

The Writer and the Writing

Is this the right time to ask for something new from the student? Look at the writer and the writing for guidance.

A. Who is this writer? _____

Based on what you have seen, assess the writer on the scales below.

Openness to new challenges:

1	2	3	4
resistant	hesitant	confident	eager

View of self as a writer:

1	2	3	4
incompetent	getting better	good	great

Do your scores fall in the 1–2 range or in the 3–4 range? The table below will give you some ideas about how best to proceed.

1–2 Range	3–4 Range
Look at what you can do. (List them) These are things good writers do. Let's look back in your book and see how far you've come! You are really coming along. Keep practising what you are doing. I am so pleased with you.	You are doing so well. You are ready to learn something new. Let me show you how to do it.

B. What's happening with the writing?

1	2	3
breaking through	getting it	consolidating it

What is your assessment of the writing? Is the timing right for instruction? See the table below for guidance.

1–2 Range	3 Range
Look at what you've done! (Describe what the writer can do. Example: You have written the longest story of your life today.) This is the best yet! I'm going to show the class what you can do now! You must be so proud.	You have learned so many things. You can _____ and _____ and _____. I think you are ready for the next step in your writing. This part of your writing sounds great because (tell why). Here's how you can make it even more powerful.

This table offers guidance in deciding the appropriate timing and content of instruction. You can read it from left to right to see the progression of skills as the child develops. If you read the continuum from top to bottom, you can see the skills that often occur together around the same time. Of course, children do not develop uniformly and some children's skills will be somewhat more diverse; however, this chart provides a general sequence for writing development and a picture of the constellation of skills at various stages. Since examples may help to make this clearer, consider the table below with two student samples in mind. The samples appear at the top of page 20.

From Scribbles to Competency: A Developmental Continuum

Stage	1	2	3	4	5	6
Picture Development	Scribbles and squiggles	Squiggles and simple representational shapes (eg., circle face)	Simple drawings with sparse details	Drawings with moderate detail depicting common events	*continues*	→
Oral Language That Precedes Writing	Labels and tells about a picture with a few words or a phrase	Tells a story in a simple sentence, adding more if prompted	Tells a simple story with a few ideas	Tells a longer story with some details	Tells a story with a beginning, middle, and end	Oral abilities continue to develop but now writing takes precedence
Hearing and Recording Sounds, Spelling	*not yet*	*not yet*	Able to hear and isolate beginning sounds Can match sound and symbol for a few initial consonants	Able to hear and isolate beginning and ending sounds Can match sound and symbol for most consonants in these positions	Uses some high-frequency words Can match sound and symbol for most consonants	Continues to represent words with consonants and may use some vowels incorrectly
Printing and Punctuation	Can print name	Left–right orientation is present with no spacing between random letter clusters	Prints mostly capitals with some small letters	Recognizes and is able to print most letters of the alphabet	Recognizes and is able to print all letters of the alphabet	Uses mixed capitals and small letters with some spacing between the "words"
Writing Development	*not yet*	Uses letters and letter strings to represent a story May label drawings with some initial consonants	Most words are represented by at least one letter	Most words are represented by at least two letters	All words are represented with some letters, but words are often omitted in sentences	Can write a complete thought with a few sight words and at least two letters representing a word Can read own writing

7	8	9	10	11	12	13
Attempting to portray actions and events beyond the everyday	*continues*		Detailed drawings with good use of color and white space	Imaginative, finely crafted drawings representing events beyond the everyday	Daily pictures discontinued as writing ability flourishes	
Continues to use vowels incorrectly Is able to write an increasing number of high-frequency words correctly	Can hear and represent more medial vowel sounds correctly	*continues*	Knows how to write more than 50 high-frequency words	Use phonics and words patterns to solve spelling problems	Knows many high-frequency words	Most high-frequency words spelled conventionally
continues	More appropriate capital use, spacing and periods show up, although not always appropriately	Uses some upper and lower case letters appropriately	Produces legible printing with letters of appropriate and uniform size	*continues*	With reminders, is able to punctuate sentences correctly and use capital letters appropriately	*continues*
Can write a complete thought	Writing can be read by others —perhaps only primary teachers!	May be a series of sentences or one very long sentence	Writes a short story that makes sense	Develops a topic with supporting details	Is able to craft writing to include emotions and dialogue Writer's voice is apparent	Is able to develop pieces of writing in varied genres, including personal narrative, poetry, non-fiction and fictional narrative Is able to use webbing and labeled diagrams to generate ideas

Sample 1
- Simple drawings with sparse detail.
- Tells a simple story with few ideas.
- Able to hear and isolate beginning sounds. Match sound-symbol for a few consonants.
- Prints mostly capitals with some small letters.
- Most words are represented by at least one letter.

Sample 2
- Drawings with moderate detail depicting common events.
- Tells a longer story with some detail.
- Able to hear and isolate beginning and ending sound-symbol for most consonants.
- Recognizes and is able to print most letters of the alphabet.
- Most words are represented by at least two letters.

In the first example, Justin tells his teacher that his story says: I soccer and I bad accident. The underlined letters represent his phonetic matches.

We can see from his first writing sample and the transcript of his story that Justin's development is represented by the section of the chart beside it. Before he has consolidated his understandings at the next level, he will be working on his picture and oral storytelling to include more details. He will continue to stretch the words and represent the sounds he hears with increasing numbers of letters. He will also build his knowledge of letters and use them in his stories.

Justin's teacher will consider all these factors when asking, "What's next for Justin?" She will aim her instruction very close to what he can do now and urge him forward a little at a time. Although we see where we need to take Justin, we understand that he cannot attend to all these skills at once. He will need time to consolidate and his teacher will provide instruction on one aspect of development at a time with at-the-elbow teaching or whole-class instruction. In that way, Justin can maintain a feeling of joy and success in writing.

In his second example, Justin tells his teacher a longer story: I see my brother and my brother is a bad guy and I fight my brother. He has expanded his story, with every word represented by at least one and often several letters and three high-frequency words used correctly. We see that Justin is moving in small increments along the continuum.

Have high expectations for effort and achievement. The perfect climate for writing is neither so demanding that children are anxious, nor so comfortable that there is no growth. In order to grow as writers, children need teachers who accept their efforts but who also prompt them to apply what they know about writing. Here some examples of classroom talk that help children to meet teacher expectations:

- I see you have a sun in your picture. Do you remember how *sun* starts? That's right—*s*. Put an *s* there by your sun. Do you hear any other sounds? Let's put them in here.

- In this part of your writing, you said you had fun. Tell me about the fun you had. What did you do? Add one of your ideas about the fun to this part of your writing.
- Remember the guidelines for writing a personal story. Check the chart and see if you have all the parts you need.

Young children can be expected to adhere to developmentally appropriate expectations. It is part of the teacher's craft to know the student well, know when a child needs support and encouragement, and know when the child needs to be held accountable to meet expectations.

One expectation is that writers will work quietly and purposefully. In a Kindergarten class, it is not possible or desirable for students to write in silence. They will be discussing their pictures and their stories as they work and those conversations help to develop their thinking. Grade 1 students, however, can be taught to sustain quiet application to their writing. Apart from vocalizing as they create sound–letter matches and using writer's mumble to read back what they have written, they should see Writing Workshop as a quiet working time. Some children do their best work when they can sit away from their classmates.

Another key expectation is that children will learn to sustain attention to their writing for increasing amounts of time. When, after a short time, children announce that they are finished, we sit with them and inquire about their stories and interests, and prompt further story development with questions that will direct them back to the writing. In addition, we make sure that the activities after Writing Workshop are not so engaging that children will rush their writing to get to other tasks. We also say, "Writing Workshop is the time for writing. We write until the time is up."

Develop criteria together. As we model in each of our Writing Workshop chapters, each mini-lesson is focused on a particular learning goal. The general goal is reflected in the chapter title, and is described in the lesson synopsis that precedes each mini-lesson. In one lesson the goal is to add detail to a picture. In another, the goal is to start with a title. In each lesson we provide a suggestion for expressing the objective of the lesson as clear criteria for student success.

We suggest that teachers make criteria charts appropriate to the age and stage of their students. These writing guides may begin in as basic a fashion as reminding students to print their names on their work—one of the most important things to learn in Kindergarten. The chart may be a pictorial representation of expectations for a story, for example, showing a bright, colorful detailed picture with some initial consonant labels. Later, the chart may show another picture with more letters in the labeling. As students progress, involve them in developing the chart. After a mini-lesson, ask: "What should we include in our writing chart today?" Make sure that the chart, usually on a large chart paper, is displayed where all students can see it, and refer to it during every mini-lesson. An example appears at the top of the next page.

> # What makes a great story from your life?
>
> ## 1. Start with a title.
> ## 2. Make all sentences belong.
> ## 3. Add personal details.
> ## 4. Use talking.
> ## 5. Show feelings.

Students find a reference like this very helpful. For very young students, the teacher might add a little picture to support each point or highlight with color a sample of text, for example, the title on a photocopied piece of work.

Sit alongside each writer. Sitting alongside the writers in the midst of Writing Workshop is a successful way to sustain engagement in writing. The teacher "works the room," pausing beside each child to talk. We take a chair around and sit at the writer's elbow, conferencing, clarifying, nudging, and encouraging the writing. Our interest helps the children to understand that writing is an important task that requires their full attention.

When we sit alongside a beginning writer, we need to make a positive response and focus on content. As children become more confident writers, our response can be more constructive, combining comments on what the child is doing well with suggestions for one or two changes.

It is important to acknowledge students who have made a good start and thought of interesting topics. For example:

"Boys and girls, as I walked around the class I noticed that Mary, Hardeep, and Gloria have all started their writing. Mary is writing about what happened this morning in the gym, Hardeep is writing about the street hockey game he played last night, and Gloria is writing about the time her Grandma took her to the restaurant. These are all good topics for a personal true-life story. Maybe their good starts will give you an idea for your writing."

Doing this can trigger other children's ideas about topics.

A few interruptions serve as reminders to the class of the elements of good writing. They acknowledge the students and highlight their skills in a positive way, encouraging them to continue with those same habits of mind. They also remind other students of what they need to do to make their writing more powerful. Then Writing Workshop settles and the teacher works quietly at the elbow of the writers.

Observe, assess, know where you are going, and plan instruction. When we sit alongside our writers, we have an opportunity to understand their beliefs about themselves as writers. We gain insight into their skill development and their needs. Anecdotal records from these conferences help us to note trends in the class and the needs of individuals or small groups of children. It is also helpful to review collections of student work to note their instructional needs.

Another useful tool is the Developmental Continuum in this book. This continuum (pages 18–19) can act as a writing profile that gives teachers a reference point and is helpful in understanding what the child has learned and where the child needs to go next. Teachers may find it helpful to use the Developmental

Chapters 1 to 22 offer direct support to the teacher for those at-the-elbow conferences. Under each work sample, there is a scenario of the interaction between the writer and the teacher.

Continuum at regular intervals throughout the year. They may staple it to a piece of writing and highlight the descriptors that apply to the writing sample. When this assessment data is collected systematically, it provides the teacher with a picture of the writer's growth over time. The teacher can use the data for planned instruction and reporting to parents.

A helpful practice is to transcribe the oral stories of very early writers whose letter strings do not yet represent words. Some teachers do this in cursive writing at the back of the child's notebook; others keep a separate record book. This transcription is *not* meant to be a model for the child; rather, it is a record of oral language development. Moreover, it demonstrates to the parent that the writing is a deliberate attempt to communicate meaning. If the teacher watches closely and asks the child to track his story with a finger as he "reads it back," she will notice when the letters start to match the story. When this occurs, she underlines the phonetic matches in the transcription. In this way, teachers and parents can see how the child is mastering the code.

Transcript of student oral story in the back of a writing book. The underlines indicate phonetic matches in the writing.

Teach explicitly. We contend that all students are ready for the right instruction: instruction that meets them at the boundaries of their independent competency and extends them, just a little, into new territory. The teacher shows the child how to do something as yet untried. In a series of supportive steps and repetition, the teacher moves the child to independence through explicit teaching. Here is the model:

Step 1: *I'll show you.* In this modeling stage in the mini-lesson, the teacher demonstrates for students by thinking aloud as she applies the skill to be learned.

Step 2: *You help me.* The teacher invites the children to join her as she prompts them to remember steps and think aloud while she models the new writing strategy with the children's assistance.

Step 3: *I'll help you.* The teacher circulates in the classroom giving at-the-elbow support as needed so that students can try the new skill for themselves.

Step 4: *Now you do it yourself.* The child has a good grasp of the skill and applies it as developmentally appropriate in his writing.

As the chart below shows, responsibility shifts gradually from teacher to student.

Model for Explicit Teaching in Writing Workshop

I'll Show You	You Help Me	I'll Help You	Now You Do It Yourself
Teacher demonstration in mini-lessons	Class participation in mini-lessons and interactive writing	At-the-elbow conferences	Independent writing
The teacher has all the responsibility for the writing.	*The teacher has the most responsibility for the writing and the children contribute as they are able.*	*The child has the most responsibility for the writing and the teacher provides support as needed.*	*The child has all the responsibility for the writing.*
Teacher Responsibility → Student Responsibility			

With these four steps, the knowledgeable teacher helps the child to move from one developmental stage to another more complex one. The context for this instruction could be one to one, as reported earlier, or in a small group, or with the whole class. Whole-class lessons form a bank of shared classroom experiences for the teacher to draw upon in at-the-elbow conferences. We follow up whole-class lessons with coaching to help young writers apply what has been demonstrated by saying, "Do you remember when we did the lesson about...?"

Chapters 1 to 22 provide guidance for teachers in knowing what to teach, when to teach it, and how it should be done. Each of these lessons presents an opportunity for the teacher to teach explicitly, *showing* students how to do it rather than *telling* them how to proceed.

Let students reflect on their learning. Allow students to reflect on the lesson and their writing experience that day. The comments they make help their classmates to learn. Through the debriefing, students gain the language to talk about their work and that, in turn, gives them metacognitive control over their strategies.

Key questions for regular writing debriefings include these:

- What helped you to do well on your writing today?
- What did you learn in your writing today?
- What will you remember to do next time?

The first question, in particular, asks students to review their strategies. They might reply:

- I just focused on my writing. I just look at my book and not at my friends.
- I had ideas in my head. I know what I want to write about.
- I had a sharp pencil ready.
- I tried my own spellings.
- I moved my hand quickly so I could write a lot.

Teach basic tools. Basic tools are the other side of the writing coin. They allow students to express their ideas effectively. Lessons focus on such topics as how to hear and represent sounds with letters, how to hold a pencil, how to form the letters and print legibly. Basic tools also encompass phonics and spelling instruction. Too much emphasis on basic tools, however, creates writing that is stiff and stilted as the child comes to believe that correct form is the most important value. We recommend that lessons in basic tools be taught explicitly outside of Writing Workshop, but reinforced one-to-one during Writing Workshop. This book focuses on lessons taught in the workshop.

"There is a distinction between what is said in writing, the composition, and what has to be done to say it, the conventions of transcription, such as spelling, punctuation, grammar and neatness. These are literally two sides of writing sometimes confused and often in opposition."

Frank Smith, *Writing and the Writer*, page 2

8. What should I do beyond Writing Workshop?

Although Writing Workshop is a time for explicit instruction that helps the writer, students need echoes of writing support and opportunities to write throughout the day. Here are some common practices that support writing:

- instruction in phonics and spelling
- phonemic awareness games, songs, rhymes, and chants
- instruction in printing
- writing in play centres—tickets, notices, signs, posters, recipes, cards
- the Morning Message, where the teacher prints a sentence or two on the chalkboard and students fill in missing letters to solve the reading puzzle
- writing in response to literature and classroom experiences
- booklet making
- opportunities for making class Big Books
- writing on the computer
- discussions about literature and the writing craft during read-aloud

The teacher can reinforce the teaching from these literacy contexts in Writing Workshop. For example, when children write about the lemonade stand during play centres, the teacher may suggest that they continue that writing during Writing Workshop. After a read-aloud the teacher could say, "Did you like that story? You might like to retell it in your writing books one day. Has anything like that ever happened to you? That would be a great topic to write about."

Another example of capitalizing on writing echoes throughout the day is to reinforce a writing skill in the Morning Message. Perhaps the teacher could illustrate an aspect of phonics introduced in a basic tools lesson or the idea of starting with a title, taught in a craft lesson. These one-minute reinforcements can do much to build layers of understanding about writing.

We also observe that when students do whole writing tasks at other times of the day, their writing improves more quickly in Writing Workshop. We urge teachers to abandon fill-in-the-blanks worksheets in favor of creating a space to write. The voice of the child needs to shape the response to the curriculum—not the computer graphics or the publisher's workbooks. You can see this reflected in the examples that follow.

Children write in response to stories read aloud:

I like the Little Red Ridinghood. I don't like the fox. The fox is bad. I like when the mom gave a basket to Little Red Riding Hood.

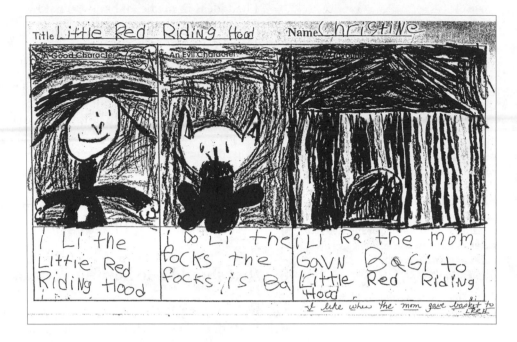

I felt happy when my mom cake and my mom kiss me. (a birthday recollection)
I felt sad when dad said go to sleep.

This story is about 16 little creatures that have to leave a tree called Shady Glade that was their home. They jumped on a train and could not jump off the train. But they found another Shady Glade and lived very happy after all.

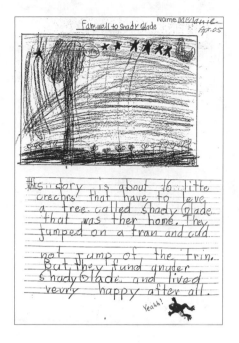

Children write to capture their understandings in science:

The plant is growing 2 stems. It is growing longer.

The snail went on the block then the snail come down to sleep.

All the mealworms went to the darkside. No mealworms went to the light side. The mealworms liked the darkside. Some of the mealworms got into the crack.

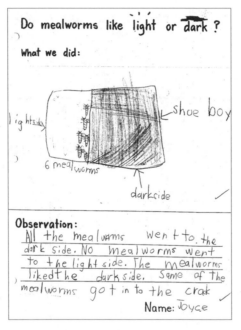

Children are led to understand that this kind of kidwriting may not contain the exact spellings of words but it can be read, and it is how students in Grade 1 do much of their writing. They need powerful words, like "incredible," "haunted," and "delicious," in their writing. They can't wait until Grade 3 to use them in their writing.

9. How should I deal with spelling?

Accept invented spelling. Invented spelling is a short-lived stage in the development of the writer. Accept children's approximations in the early stages to help them work with confidence in the Learning Zone and grow as writers. Invented spellings, what we often call *kidwriting*, are often delightful and form the very essence of a young writer's voice and expression. Understand that this is a fleeting stage and have faith that students will move beyond it.

Teach phonemic awareness, phonics, and spelling rules. Time your instruction appropriately so that children learn tools to spell with increasing accuracy.

Children who have well-developed sound–letter matches and are able to represent every word with one or more letters are ready to be introduced to a few high-frequency words. The number of high-frequency words a child is expected to know increases as the child masters phonetic conventions.

In Writing Workshop, we ask children to stretch out the sounds in a word, to feel the sounds in their mouths, to listen to them with their ears, and then to write down the letters that make those sounds. It is sometimes helpful to call this slow and soft sounding out "ghost talk." Children will gradually go from hearing and recording only one or two sounds to making more sound–letter matches until they are beginning to have a legible piece of writing.

Although we expect children to stretch out words as they are writing, it is helpful to provide some practice and support for the difficult job of isolating phonemes. Marie Clay, in her Reading Recovery program, suggests that using Elkonin sound boxes to help children hear and record the sounds in words creates an excellent bridge between listening to the sounds in words and writing those words. It is a strategy for young children who have a number of sound–symbol matches, but need practice putting it all together, perhaps over a number of days.

Hold students increasingly accountable, but determine expectations for spelling accuracy child by child. Expectations for spelling accuracy increase as the year progresses; the teacher applies her knowledge of the developmental needs of each child. By the end of Grade 1, most children will be able to spell correctly if the word

- is easily visible in the classroom
- is a high-frequency word that has been taught
- is phonetically reliable (e.g., thing, shot, porch) and the phonemes have been taught

Good practical reminders are small spelling references pasted in the front of the writing book or three or four words written on Post-its on the child's desk for reference for the week.

Thoughtful teachers may use the time they sit alongside young writers to help them remember the spelling rules they know and apply them in their work. The corrections are made by the child with the teacher's support. You can see this demonstrated in the lessons that follow—the teacher does not take the book away and "mark it" for spelling errors.

A word of caution: Use spelling references, such as dictionaries and word walls, sparingly.

In our experience, using spelling references can lead children to believe that perfect spelling has greater value than expression. Moreover, we find that word walls are the least helpful for those that need them most—too many words, too far away. Children may also use spelling references as "writing avoidance" tactics.

Introduction to what's next

We have shown how to conduct a Writing Workshop in which students feel supported and sustain writing for extended periods of time. We have shown how to encourage writers to find ideas for stories and to take risks with language. We have provided guidance on how to work with spelling, how to teach the whole

Using an Elkonin Box

1. **Move it and say it.**
   Students place tokens or pennies below each box and, and as they slowly stretch out a word like s-p-o-t, move the penny into the box above sound by sound.
2. **Say it slowly and write it.**
   Students put a letter or letters into each box to record the sound they hear. Doing this provides a visual and tactile dimension to isolating phonemes. It helps students who may have difficulty hearing and recording all the sounds in words as they say the word slowly.

The goal: To have students write the letters as they hear the sounds in their head

group, and how to work the room sitting beside each writer for coaching and encouragement.

In the following chapters, you will find student samples that follow a continuum of writing development. We start with writers who are able to make scribbles and squiggles on a page, engage in a limited oral discussion about their work, and print their name. We take them to the beginnings of fluency, crafting their writing in four genres, and using writing to communicate meaning across the curriculum. In each chapter we offer language to affirm the child's efforts and a suggestion for moving the child to the next step of writing development.

Depending on the child, the time span represented in the following chapters will vary from a few months to three years and beyond. In our experience, it represents the "typical" development of writers in Kindergarten and Grade 1. Some teachers may think, *But my students are ESL!* Many of the samples come from children who entered Kindergarten in East Vancouver with limited English ability. (See the Appendices for tips on helping ESL students.) Just see what they can do!

The lessons in Chapters 1 to 22 represent our best attempt to help teachers of writing as they pose the final question:

What's next for this beginning writer?

Pages 111 and 112 consist of a brochure, i Kn rit, which can be photocopied back to back and folded. The brochure presents a summary of the early stages of writing development. It is a useful reference for teachers and families.

Chapter One: Making a Picture That Tells a Story

Celebrating success	Eric, you've been working hard on this picture. Look at your colors. What does this say? Eric, I like how you have written your name. I can read it. Tell me a story about your picture.
Extending the language	I see your house, Eric. It's green and it's a rectangle shape.
Extending the writing	Can you tell me more about your story of you and your house? *I play with my brother.* Where can you make that part of the story? You could draw your brother right here. (Eric draws a few more scribbles.) *This is my brother.*
Setting a goal	Remember when you draw your story you tell about things you do. Now, your story tells about you and your brother. Tomorrow you can make a picture that tells a story.

Identifying the Need

Children's first experiences with writing are often squiggles and scribbles, much as Eric's sample. Eric, however, has the fine-motor skills to craft his name and should be able to make more representational and detailed drawings. As you model writing about shared and individual experiences and classroom events, you will find that this lesson needs much repeating.

Getting Ready

- Post a large blank piece of paper on the chalkboard or chart stand.

Teaching the Lesson

1. Tell the students that you are going to show them how to develop a picture like a writer. You might sound like this: "Today you will be writers and you are going to have a special time called Writing Workshop where you will draw and write a story about something interesting that you did or saw."

2. Talk out loud to demonstrate the thinking required in creating a story. It might go something like this:

   "Uum! I have to make a story. I have to think about what I have done or seen that was kind of interesting. I know! I saw an eagle fly up to his nest in the tree and I just bet there were baby eagles in there! The eagle had something in his mouth—it might have been a fish because it was right near the water."

3. Draw the components of the story, using different colors and keeping shapes simple. The process would go something like this:

   "What did what I saw look like? Well, there was a big tree. I'll make it tall and show its long branches and leaves. There was a nest. It was shaped like this. I really have to think carefully about the shape. I couldn't see the babies. Then along came the eagle. He is kind of an oval shape with a round head and really wide wings. They were so big! Now I saw something in his mouth. I'll make a little shape like a triangle for a beak and have something hanging down. Eagles have sharp eyes. I better make his eye. The tree was by the ocean. I'll make waves and make the water blue. But of course, the tree was on the land. Here's how I made the ground. The ground is brown. The sun was shining . . ."

   Be sure to emphasize using the white space, including details, drawing big, and making the picture bright and colorful.

4. When the simple picture is done, tell a story two or three sentences long.

5. Ask the students to tell their partners the story.

6. Demonstrate writing your story with the picture, placing the story on the bottom of the paper: *I saw an eagle fly up to his nest. I think that he has babies in his nest.*

7. Ask students to think about what they have done or seen lately that they found interesting. You might help them visualize being in their house, on the street,

---

Sidebar notes:

Although improvement in drawing happens naturally as students mature, it is helpful to model drawing some simple shapes and figures in a step-by-step format to encourage students to draw more proficiently.

Making a strong statement with a crayon is the first step in risk taking in writing. We encourage children to remember the 3 Bs: Big, Bold, Bright.

This is not the time to teach beginning sounds, capitals, spacing, and so on. The focus needs to be on the thinking process for picture and story making.

or at school when something interesting happens. Tell them to raise a hand when they have a good idea for a story and share some responses.

8. Ask students to tell a partner about their story.

> *"Think about three or four things you will draw to make your story interesting. Let's see, I drew a tree, a bird, the water, and a sun. Count on your fingers. Now what four things will you draw? Tell your partner about those things. Use your fingers to help you."*

9. Ask students to draw and write their story. Remind them that you want to see four things!

Building Criteria
- **Print your name.**
- **Make a picture.**
- **"BBB"**
- **Make letters.**

Prompting Student Review

- Can you tell a story about your picture?

Monitoring Student Progress

- Did the student choose three or four different shapes of things in their drawing?
- Is there improvement in their ability to draw representational figures?
- Is the student included in the story?
- Was there good use of color and white space?

Chapter Two: Telling a Story from a Picture

Celebrating success	Abby, I like the way that you have made so many things in your picture. I see the sun and rainbow, the house and flowers. You are remembering that your picture tells a story, and this one seems very bright and happy. You remembered the 3 Bs! Tell me about your story.
Extending the language	*This is my house and my yard.* I like the way your house has two big windows to look out. What do you see when you look out your windows? *I see the street.*
Extending the writing	If you were in this story, Abby, what might you be doing? What interesting thing? *I might be helping my mom pick some flowers.* Do you think you can put you and your mom in this picture? What will you write? *My mom and me are picking flowers.* Let's make some letters and letter shapes that tell that story.
Setting a goal	Tomorrow when you do your writing, make some letters and letter shapes that tell the story. Pretend that you can write.

Identifying the Need

Before children can write a story, they have to be able to tell it. This lesson emphasizes the oral part of the writing process. It might be done in part after you have read a wonderful picture book and want children to tell the story from the pictures or when children come in with a picture from a newspaper and tell the story behind the photo. It is best done when it relates to pictures that students have drawn themselves.

Getting Ready

- Select three or four pictures from the children's drawings.
- Make the pictures into overheads or enlarge them so they are Big Book size.

Teaching the Lesson

1. Tell the students, "Today you are going to learn to be authors. Authors write their stories so everyone can hear them and remember them." You might hold up a familiar picture book, such as *Mr. Gumpy's Outing* by John Burningham, that illustrates this principle.

2. Choose one of the overhead pictures and demonstrate the thinking process that matches story to picture. It might sound like this: "I am going to show you how to use this picture to tell a great story. First, you have to look for details in the picture. Label four or five things that you see in the story."

3. Talk out loud about the possibilities of a story. "Hmm! What kind of story can I tell with this picture? It should be interesting! I know. First, I'll tell about the people." (Say the sentence out loud and then print it quickly on chart paper, the board, or the overhead.) "Then I'll tell about what they are doing." (Say it out loud and write.) "Now what else do I see in this picture that I can tell about?" (Add one more sentence.)

4. Move on to the second picture and engage the students in developing the story together in a similar manner. "What do you see in the picture? What are the people doing? Use your imagination to tell a story about the picture."

At this stage, just write and keep your talk about conventions brief. This time is for thinking through story, not learning about beginning sounds!

5. Write the story on the board as the students tell it. Ask them to use their imaginations to contribute sentences until you have a three- or four-sentence story.

6. With the third picture, ask students to tell their partner about what they see. Then ask them to think of a story that tells about the picture. Prompt with questions if they need it, for example: "What do you see in the picture? What are the people doing? Where are you? Who are the people in the story? What is happening? How do you feel?"

Remind students that if they don't know the words they should make some letters and letter shapes to represent them.

7. Praise their good efforts.

8. Ask students to think about what they will draw. Elicit some responses. Tell them to go to their seats, draw a picture, and be ready to tell a story about it.

Prompting Student Review

• Who are the characters in your story?
• Can you tell me a long story about what they are doing?

Monitoring Student Progress

• Is the student able to tell a story with characters?
• Is the student able to tell a story that matches the picture?
• Does at least one interesting thing happen in the story?

Chapter Three: Finding Words and Letters Around the Room

Celebrating success	Jasmine, you have done such a pretty picture. You have lots of details and I think that this girl is doing something interesting. Can you tell me this story?
Extending the language	*This is my Mom. She is by the tree and she is happy.* I could tell she was happy by her smile. I love her beautiful yellow dress. Can you tell me about your happy mother?
Extending the writing	Tell me about your writing. Read it to me. *Mom.* Wow! That is absolutely right. Now, how did you know how to make that word? *It is up there in the family chart.* That's right. We can use words we see in our room and we can think of letters we know to make writing. You did a smart thing!
Setting a goal	Are there other words you know that you can see in our room? *I know the words "Dad," "the" and "Janie."* Well, you can use those words in your stories. Don't forget to use the words in the room to help your writing.

Identifying the Need

The first words that children learn to read and write often have significant meaning to them. *Mom, Dad,* their name and those of family members are typical firsts. When students are learning how to read and write sight words, words found in sentence starters like *I love … I like … I can …* seem easily learned. These words are often found in classrooms where student art and classroom books are on display. These classrooms also have many posters, Big Books, word walls, classroom labels, graphs, and chart stories for children to use as they begin to write.

Teach this lesson now because students understand that Writing Workshop is a time for making a picture, telling the story with details, and writing words. Since many students at this time do not have either the phonetic skills to make accurate sound–symbol matches or the spelling knowledge to write words they want, we encourage them to write by printing letters they know, or if they like, copying some words from around the room.

This activity helps children see themselves as real authors writing their stories, or "kidwriting." Kidwriting is explained to children as the kind of writing done before they know how to make all the words.

> It's important to note that this is a "bridging" strategy. We want students to move quickly from this stage to hearing and recording sounds in words.

Teaching the Lesson

1. Engage students in discussion of a writing dilemma. It might sound like this:

   > *"Today I am going to pretend that I am a Kindergarten student just like you. I am doing Writing Workshop, but I have a big problem! I want you to listen carefully and see if you can help me solve my problem.*

   > *"I am going to make a story about building a snowman. I am building it in my yard and the sun is shining, and I know I have to have lots of details."*

2. Continue on like this until you have sketched a quick scene, then say: "Now, I have to write my story at the bottom. But I don't know how to make a story." (Make a sad face.) "I only know how to make my name! What shall I do?"

3. Elicit solutions from students, who might say something like, "Just pretend you are writing!"

4. Continue in this manner. Again, students will probably suggest looking at the alphabet chart, looking at their names. and so on.

5. Model matching letters and sounds for one word."Okay, I'm going to make my story with pretend writing. I will make some of my favorite letters." (Print some random letters and tell where you got them.) "Oh, and I need to have snow in my story, and here is the word 'snow' on the weather chart. I'll just make it the same. Let's see, first an s, then an n, and then an o, and a w on the end. Hey! That was smart."

6. Discuss with students where words and letters are found in the classroom and make a list of where to look.

7. Engage students in a game as follows:

"Okay, let's play this game with our partners. One of you is sad and has a problem. Let's hear you say, 'I can't write!' Now, your partner will tell you where to look and where you can find letters and words for your story."

Help the students role-play by having one of the partners demonstrate having the problem and the other student offering solutions. Later, have partners switch roles. Emphasize that in Writing Workshop, they can find letters and words around the room to help them write their stories.

Prompting Student Review

• Can you tell me your story?
• What "pretend writing" did you do for your story?

Monitoring Student Progress

• Are students able to make some letters and letter shapes to represent writing?
• Are some students able to use copied words in their story in a meaningful way?

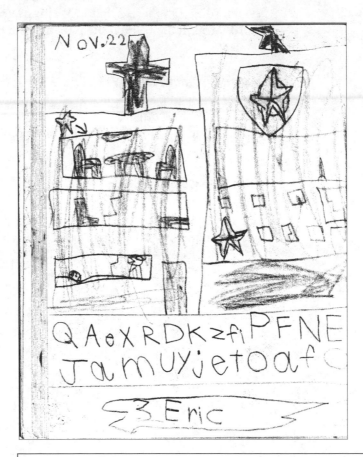

Celebrating success	Eric, this picture is so detailed. I can hardly wait to hear your story. You have so many things to tell about in this picture. Look at all your wonderful writing. You have made a long story. Tell it to me. *The police are in the house and the dentist is downstairs.*
Extending the language	Can you tell me about the police? Why are they in the house? *The people upstairs are shouting bad words.* Oh! That sounds scary! Does this badge tell where they are? *Yes.* Tell me more about the dentist. *Someone is looking sad. That's a boy who has a toothache and the dentist is going to fix it.* Tell me about how this boy is feeling.
Extending the writing	Can you read your writing for me? Show me where you will start? (Eric points to the Q.) *This is a house and this is a police station.* You have told your story in two ways, one with the picture and one with the letters.
Setting a goal	I like the way you made this arrow with the badge to show where the police are. I wonder if we can make the word "police." Let's get our mouth ready to say "Police." What sound does it start with? *Pp.* Do you know the letter that makes that sound? Why don't we put it beside the badge? How about the dentist? What sound does the word "dentist" start with? *Dd.* Where can we put that? Tomorrow we can put in some of the letters that tell about the things in your story.

Identifying the Need

It is good practice to encourage children to write the date at the top of their page. The dates show how much their writing is improving over time. The practice provides an easy way for children to make meaningful letters as well as help order their work. Provide the date for them and show how it might be recorded on the top left side.

Early exposure to these expected behaviors helps young students begin to develop good work habits.

Good teachers always "talk with their chalk." Long before children can read print, teachers are putting up lists, labeling quickly sketched diagrams, making columns, and creating Venn diagrams to sort and show similarities and differences. This, at the very least, demonstrates to children the connection between thinking and recording those thoughts with print and diagrams. For the students in the class who are already reading, it provides reinforcement and stimulation at the appropriate level. As for students just beginning to break the code, they observe and learn an amazing amount. As children get older, these visual aids provide an important way for them to make good connections.

This explicit lesson focuses on the use of labeling what students draw or see in pictures. Labeling is a less complex task than creating the story in sentence form, but reinforces the idea that a picture tells a story. Using labels helps students feel in control of their writing and is developmentally appropriate at a time when putting together a sentence using sound–symbol connections might be too difficult for them.

Getting Ready

- Create a couple of overheads from student pictures or draw pictures of your own.
- Display a simple picture book that contains labels to illustrate how authors use labels to tell part of the story. Recommended titles include any books by Gail Gibbons and *The Word Book* by Richard Scarry.

Teaching the Lesson

In Eric's work on the previous page, there is a sophisticated drawing, but the story consists of a string of random letters. Eric was redirected to use phonemes he knows to describe his picture.

1. Tell the students, "Sometimes when we make a picture and write our story, we need to think about the letters that match the words. We can start by finding the letters that match the sounds of words in our picture."

   Note: In Kindergarten the word "story" refers to anything students write, whether it is non-fiction, personal narrative, or fantasy.

2. Show students the first picture which should display at least four items. Tell your story about the picture, point to each object, and write down the sounds you hear with an arrow pointing to the object.

3. For the next picture, engage the students in suggesting ideas for the story and identifying the objects. Prompt them to describe who is in the story, what is happening, and what objects they see.

4. Choose some objects to label and ask students to listen for sounds as they stretch out the words. Advise them that it doesn't always have to be the beginning sound, just any sound in the word.

5. Ask students to find a picture they drew in their writing books. Ask them to choose an object in the picture and say the word it represents slowly stretching out the sounds. See if they can put a letter that matches a sound they hear. Show them how to make an arrow go from the letter to the object.

Labeling is a transitional step that helps some children connect sound, symbol, picture, and story. We would not include it on a criteria chart.

6. Now, ask students to proceed with their own pictures for story writing. Prompt them to include some initial consonants with their pictures.

7. Circulate, stopping to have at-the-elbow conferences with students. In each conference, help the child to hear, name, and represent the initial sounds for items in the pictures.

Prompting Student Review

- Show me some letters that match some of the things in your picture.
- Tell me a story about your picture.
- Where is your writing for your story?

Monitoring Student Progress

- What sound–symbol connections, if any, are students making in their labeling?
- Do students place letters and arrows to show they understand the concept of labeling?
- Are students able to tell stories about their pictures?

Abby's art shows attempts at labeling: H for house, F for flowers, and A for Abby. Her story: Abby is picking flowers by her house.

Chapter Five: Writing at the Bottom of the Page

Little rainbow, flower, mountain, ground. The girl is climbing to the top of the mountain.

Celebrating success	Abby, let me tell you why this picture makes me know that you are doing some good learning. First, you have five bright and beautiful colors; you have details like clouds, a rainbow, mountains, flowers and a very brave girl on top of the mountain. You have worked hard on your writing with lots of letters that label the things in your picture. Tell me about your writing and your pictures.
Extending the language	The girl is a mountain climber! What do you think she might need to help her climb the mountain? Can you read me your words?
Extending the writing	I am so proud of you! You have found lots of the sounds in the words you are writing. I love the way you did *GAN* for ground. You heard that *n*. You found three sounds in little, and you found the word "flower" up on the chart and copied it! Good for you. Do you think we can make our story at the bottom like the one in the books we've been reading? What will it say? *The girl sees a little rainbow on top of the mountain.*
Setting a goal	Tomorrow, try making a story at the bottom of the page.

Identifying the Need

Some teachers like students at this level to draw and color on the right-hand page, and make their stories on the left-hand page. Although this practice solves many problems related to organization, it does take a lot of paper!

Students at this stage in their development are ready to make a story that looks like sentences at the bottom of the page. Since many students at this stage are using a blank book for writing, or blank pages for a portfolio, it is useful to teach them how to organize their page to allow ample room for a great picture and a story. They can look at formats published authors use and come to better understand that the writing tells the story. This lesson helps to establish top-bottom, left-right orientation for young students.

Teachers know how important the organization of a page is. They often help children organize the space for their writing by drawing a pencil line to separate story and picture, sometimes drawing lines for children to print on. We know that teaching children to find the bottom of the page for themselves and estimating how much room they will need to write a story will let them have independent control and save teacher preparation time. Some children will need assistance, but many can handle this easily on their own with good instruction and practice.

Getting Ready

- Select a number of simple children's books that illustrate the concept of a story at the bottom of the page, as well as some that have story on one page, picture on the other.
- Set a large sheet of unlined paper on the board or chart stand and place colored markers ready.

Teaching the Lesson

1. Tell the children about using the space on the page to write a story. It might sound like this: "Today you will learn about one way of planning what a picture book looks like. This will be useful because we are all authors and we can use this plan in our books."

2. Point to your large piece of paper and say, "Today you will need to answer some questions about where things are and will need some words to help you." Then, put your finger on the top of the page, the bottom, the left-hand side, and the right-hand side, asking "Where am I pointing?" each time.

3. Make sure children know the vocabulary of position. Top, bottom, middle, left-hand side, right-hand side, near the bottom, near the top, in the middle. Let children use hand signals, unison response, and Yes/No (thumbs up or down) as you practise and check for understanding.

4. Do a "Talking Out Loud" as an author, trying to decide where to put the story and the writing. "Should I put the story in the middle and the picture here? Maybe I should put the story on top and the picture underneath?" (Pretend confusion.) "What can I do to help me solve my problem? I know!" (Point to books along the chalk ledge). "I'll look at what these authors have done! You can look with me!"

5. Look through the pre-selected books and discover that often the writing of the story goes near the bottom of the page, although not always!

6. At their seats, have students open their writing books and ask them to point to the areas you ask for, such as top of page, near the top, near the bottom, left-hand side, and right-hand side. Check for understanding.

7. Tell students they need to think about whether their story will be long or short before they start to write. Ask them to place a dot near the left-hand side where they think they should begin to write their story. Show them that it should be near the bottom of the page. You might want to have them draw a light line above that dot so they know where the bottom of their picture will be. Be sure to demonstrate on your white paper.

8. Remind children of these criteria for a good picture: lots of details, big, bold, bright colors, use of all the white space. Demonstrate on your white paper by sketching a picture of a story you are thinking of. Make a one-sentence story about your picture on the paper, discussing where to begin, what direction to go, and spacing between words.

9. Remind the students that today you want to see a story that is printed in a straight line going from left to right, near the bottom of the page. There should be spaces between words. Remind them that they can use kidwriting if they want. Review the order in which you want children to set up their pages, including date at top, dot for beginning of story, and line drawn at the bottom of picture. Engage children in a brief discussion of story topics and let them get started.

Building Criteria
• **Print under your picture.**

Prompting Student Review

• Can you show me where your writing is?
• Is your writing near the bottom of the page?
• Read your story. Did you make some matches with the sounds in the words?

Monitoring Student Progress

• Was the student able to organize the page appropriately?
• Did writing proceed in a left-to-right direction near the bottom of the page?
• Was this a difficult task for the student?

Chapter Six: Reinforcing the Learning—Making Stories from Pictures

It is now time to consolidate the mini-lessons students have had so far in Writing Workshop. They have been learning how to

- draw a picture with details
- tell an oral story about their picture that contains more than one idea
- organize a page that tells a story and contains some "writing"

Students may print a string of letters and letter shapes on the page or be able to make sound–symbol matches as they print letters to label their pictures or tell their stories.

In the classroom, the teacher continues to model story writing skills daily as well as introduce some writing conventions, such as

- left-right orientation
- use of capitals, periods, and spaces, especially during interactive writing with the students
- phonemic awareness and sound–symbol matching

Throughout the day, children use their kidwriting to respond to the curriculum. At the building centre, they make signs; in the home centre, they can use pencil and paper for shopping lists and menus. They respond to the literature they hear with pictures and stories that show their critical thinking. In math they count, sort, and make graphs with words.

All of these opportunities for learning have impact on Writing Workshop. In Writing Workshop, the teacher refers to them often as models for good writing behavior during at-the-elbow conferences. For example, as a child struggles to make the word "bridge," the teacher might say, "Do you remember the sign Tommy and you made at the Block Centre? You put a sign on the bridge. What letter did it start with?" In this way teachers are able to prompt so that a student might come up with the answer himself rather than being told.

In the following examples, the teacher is responding to the children and making some decisions about what's next for the beginning writers. The teacher is careful to reinforce what the child already knows and make a simple goal that is easily attainable in the next few days of Writing Workshop.

Two policemen found the bad guy.

Celebrating success	Wow, Eric, I am looking forward to hearing this story. I like the way you have used your white space, put your date on top, and included all these details. Tell me your story.
Extending the language	That sounds pretty exciting. Can you tell me what happened? *The bad guy is robbing a store.* Tell me more! *The police will get him to jail.* I like this long story, You told me that two police officers found the bad guy. The bad guy was robbing a store and the police are going to take the bad guy to jail. Is that right?
Extending the writing	I like your writing. Let me read it. (Pointing at each letter for each word) "Two policemen found [the] bad guy." You are doing a smart thing. You are making the sounds in your mouth and printing them down here. I see f for found, and b for bad and g for guy. You made the right matches! Let's see what else we can do. Let's stretch out the word b—a—d. Here is the B; can you hear another sound? *D-d-d.* Sometimes we can make two sounds we hear for a word. We can put bd for bad. How about guy? You say it slow, g-i. What other sound do you hear? *I.* Great. Where can you put it?
Setting a goal	Remember we can listen for more than one sound in some of our words. Be sure to do that next time you write.

What's next? Finding more sounds in words

Celebrating success	Queenie, I'm interested in your picture. This looks very spooky! I like all your details, and I can read this word. It says "Boo!" Good for you, can you tell me the whole story? *I am going trick-or-treating. I am a ghost. I get candy.*
Extending the language	Where is this little ghost going? What kind of weather is it outside? What do you think the jack-o-lantern is thinking?
Extending the writing	I like this word you wrote. Boo! It looks like a label, but it works like a talking bubble too! Let's think of more words to tell about your picture. You could write *ghost*. What sounds do you hear?
Setting a goal	We can make some labels for our story by saying the words and listening for the sounds,

What's next? Making labels

I watched the leaf fall down.

Celebrating success	When I saw this picture I had so many questions. It made me so interested! I asked myself, "Why is the girl lying on the ground?" I wonder what the author says. Then I looked at the story the author had written and I saw two familiar words: "the leaf." Can you tell me the whole story?
Extending the language	Tell me about the leaf. Did the leaf knock you over and make you fall down too? What did it feel like to lie in the grass and look at the sky and the leaves?
Extending the writing	You worked so hard on your writing. I like the way you looked at the board and copied the words "the leaf" and used them in your writing! That is a smart way to learn to write! And here you made *fall down* by stretching out the words. What a good job!
Setting a goal	Usually authors make their stories by putting them on the bottom of the page. Do you remember how we learned to do it? You make a dot above the bottom of the page and then make a line above the dot that will be the bottom of your picture. Do that tomorrow. Here's a sticky note with a dot and a line to remind you.

What's next? Organizing so that the writing is below the picture

Sample Consolidation Lesson

Time	Purpose	Writing Workshop Activity
5 minutes	Provide a warm-up.	"Today you are going to help me do Writing Workshop. My page is open. My crayons and pencil are ready. What will I need to do first? That's right. I need to think about something interesting to write about. Who can help me? Before I write I need to organize my page. Where will I put the date? Where will my writing start? I'll put a dot here and a line to show where my picture will end."
5 minutes	Model putting up details in the picture as rehearsal for writing.	"Today I am going to write about playing ball with my friend in the school-yard. What will I draw? Here is the school and here is the big field. I am standing by the tree and my friend is over by the fence. There are other students playing, and I think I'll even put the cement with the hopscotch in my picture. Let's see. Do I have at least four details?"
2 minutes	Model thinking about printing.	"Now, I have to write words. I might have to use kidwriting because I have to stretch out my sounds. I'm going to ask you to help me write my story. What shall I say?" (Elicit a sentence like "I like to play ball with my friend.") "Okay, where will I start?"
8 minutes	Model writing the sentence in kidwriting and let children write some of the story.	"I have to repeat the sentence in my head so I will remember it, 'I like to play ball with my friend.' Who can write I for me? Now what do I have to do before I write the next word? That's right, I need to make a space. The next word is like ... Let's say it slowly. Let's everyone say the first letter out loud. Yes, it's L. Who can hear the next letter?" (Continue until you have "I lik to pla bl." You can tell them that this is kidwriting, and then show them the standard writing; erase it quickly, though, because the emphasis is on kidwriting.)
30 minutes	Students think of a topic, draw a picture, and compare stories.	"Now, it's your turn to find a topic. Let's hear your ideas." (Students contribute a number of ideas.)
5 minutes	Recap the lesson.	• Who remembered to make a picture with lots of details? • Who organized their page? • Who remembered to start near the bottom at the left-hand side of the page? • Who used some kidwriting? • Show your partner all the things you did today in Writing Workshop. • Give yourself a clap for all your hard work.

Chapter Seven: Telling a Story with Kidwriting

It is sunny. I am happy. I am playing.

Celebrating success	Abby, what a long story you have made to go with your picture! Let's see if I can read it. It is sunny. (Pointing to each word) I am happy. I am playing. Did I read it right? *Yes.* You are such a good writer!
Extending the language	Tell me more about this happy girl who is playing. Who is she playing with? What game is she playing? Where is she? I need to know more! *She is playing outside at recess with Jasmine.*
Extending the writing	Hmm! I hear your story. She is playing outside at recess with Jasmine. Look how many details you gave me! I know where she is and who she is playing with. Good writers tell people what is happening in the story and where the story is. That is a good story!
Setting a goal	Tomorrow when you write your story, it might tell me some details. I'm looking forward to seeing your long story tomorrow!

Identifying the Need

As students learn more about sound–symbol matches and begin to experiment with known sight words like *Mom*, *and*, and *the*, they are demonstrating readiness for creating a written story with invented spellings that contain more than one sound for each word. Many students, however, may be getting the message from home or elsewhere that words should be spelled in standard accurate form. This lesson reinforces students' belief that they have licence to experiment with sounds and letters: that *kidwriting* is what to do until they know how to spell lots of words and that it follows the form of standard writing with capitals at the beginning, spaces between words, and periods at the end. Children need to have some basis of alphabetic understanding before they recognize the difference between kidwriting and conventional writing.

Getting Ready

- Assemble four enlarged pictures of typical story events, preferably from the students' own work, or from large paintings or pictures they have done.
- Obtain one felt pen or crayon for each team of five students.
- Prepare three long sentence strips for each team to be handed out one at a time.

Teaching the Lesson

1. Organize the students into five-member teams.

2. Tell the students, "Today we are going to learn more about kidwriting. Before, we talked about pretend writing and said we could find letters and words around the room to help us make our stories. Most writers, however, think up the words in their heads and stretch out the words and print the letters from the sounds they have in their mouths. Today we are going to practise making our stories from our heads."

3. Present the first picture and say, "I will tell you a story about this picture. The girl is at home. Today I am going to make short stories, but I hope you will make longer ones!"

   Printing on an eraseable board or chalk board, go through the writing steps. "Where will I start? First, I need a capital. What will I put down for the word 'the.' Since this is a sight word I usually say, that's a word we all know. Who can spell it?" Get student responses to help make all the other words: The grl is at hom.

4. Tell the students that this is kidwriting, what they do when they are kids, then show them what the sentence looks like in standard writing. Print, "The girl is at home." Explain that this is how their parents and older sisters and brothers write, but that they are not expected to do it yet. Kidwriting is what students in Kindergarten and Grade 1 do!

5. Count the words in the story together. Emphasize that there are five words and five children on each team. Ask children to repeat the sentence and tell them they will need to remember it to write it on their strips.

Many of these lessons suggest enlarging student work to the 11 x17 size of paper. With almost all of our schools having copiers with enlargers, this task is no longer difficult. Students love to see their work enlarged. It gives them an opportunity to take pride in their work and have it celebrated by their peers. Making enlargements is one small way teachers can celebrate the successes of their students.

It is hard for young children to listen to a lesson and not take the top off the felt pen, or lift up their sentence strip, or even worse, crinkle it! To avoid these distractions, do not pass out the felt pens or sentence strips until students are ready to begin writing in their teams.

6. Erase the story. Ask the teams to write the story in kidwriting. Each person on the team will write one word, remembering to put spaces between the words, and then hand the pen to another student. The other team players can help.

7. Dictate the sentence for the teams to print: The girl is at home.

8. Repeat the process with two more pictures.

- With student help, write the story shown by the picture in kidwriting. Aim to hear and record at least two sounds in each word.
- Show them what the sentence looks like in standard writing.
- Count the number of words, and repeat the sentence until they have it in their heads.
- Erase the board and prompt groups to write it on their sentence strips by using their sounds, or kidwriting.
- Dictate the sentence for the teams to print.

You may need one team to demonstrate the activity, depending on the competencies of the class. Accept all approximations; don't expect them to be the same as yours!

Building Criteria
- Use kidwriting—print the sounds you hear.

Prompting Student Review

- Tell me your story.
- Show me where you did kidwriting.
- Read this kidwriting to me.

Monitoring Student Progress

- Is there evidence of left-right orientation, as well as use of capitals, periods, and spacing?
- Are there more sound–symbol matches?
- Can the students "read" back their kidwriting with accuracy?

Left:
One bad guy. One good guy.

—*by Eric*

Right:
I pick a pumpkin. I see a rainbow.

—*by Queenie*

Chapter Eight: Putting More Detail in Pictures

I like to catch insects.

Celebrating success	Markus, when you read your sentence to me I see that you know how to match so many sounds and letters. You have even used *ch* for catch. Well done!
Extending the language	I am so interested in hearing about the insects you catch. What kinds do you like to catch? Where do you go to catch them? Do you catch them in a bottle?
Extending the writing	Markus, you have told me about so many bugs. You have told me about catching them in the tall grass and looking under rocks and stumps. Where could you draw those things in your picture? I'd like to see more about your insect adventure.
Setting a goal	When you are drawing tomorrow, try to imagine all the things around you in the place where your story is happening. Imagine the things you see there and put them in your picture.

Identifying the Need

By this time, students are thinking of a myriad of events about which to write stories, and they are often anxious to get their drawings done and move on to their writing. When writing is beginning to flow, more time should be set aside for Writing Workshop. Nonetheless, the picture remains the stimulus needed to help the students organize their thinking.

The ability to visualize is critical to good authorship. Here, students are asked to think critically about the "moment" or event that encompasses their story. They are encouraged to visualize the scene and consider all that they see around them: the objects and the behaviors of the people.

Getting Ready

- Prepare a minimal picture with a stick figure and a lot of white space.
- Write a five- or six-sentence story describing an event in your life.

Teaching the Lesson

1. Ask students to look at the picture and read the story aloud with the class.

2. Engage students in a discussion about the picture and the story, and tell them that the two are supposed to be related. Ask, "What is missing in this picture?" Tell them to pretend they are the person in the picture and if using the example at left, have them shut their eyes and whisper to themselves all the things they see at the Aquatic Centre. They might suggest the slide, the waves, the friends, the diving board, all the people. As they make suggestions, add these details to the picture.

3. Explain to students that they will get ideas for their writing if they close their eyes and go back to the time and place. Their goal is to put all the details in the picture.

    Before students begin to write, ask them to close their eyes and "see" the time and place where their stories are set today. Direct students to think of three or four details to put in their pictures.

4. Model aloud for students. For example:

    "I am going to write about my birthday party. When I close my eyes I can see a chocolate cake and five cards on the shelf. I can see my family at the table and a big sign that says, 'Happy Birthday.' I will draw all those details in my picture."

5. Ask children to share their details of time and place with a partner, then tell them to include all of them when they draw their pictures. If they forget, encourage them to close their eyes and imagine.

6. Once students have finished their pictures, ask them to leave their writing books open on their desks. Take a gallery walk, follow-the-leader style, to see all the pictures in the class and look at all the details students have put in their work.

Sample Story
I went to the Aquatic Centre yesterday. I played in the wave pool with my friends. I slid down the twisty slide. I jumped off the diving board. There were lots of people at the pool.

Ulla finds that the students entering Grade 1 are increasingly well prepared and competent. She now gives them a choice, quite early in the year, to draw their pictures with pencil instead of crayons. When sketching with a pencil, children often include more detail and are better able to keep their topics in mind. Later in the year, many children stop drawing because they have learned how to rehearse for writing mentally.

Building Criteria
- Visualize the details and then draw your picture.

Prompting Student Review

- Tell me how you can help yourself remember details for your pictures.
- What will you remember to do before you write now?

Monitoring Student Progress

- Is the student able to show three or four details in the drawings?
- Is the student able to expand the story by giving details of time and place?

Chapter Nine: Putting More Detail in Writing

Yesterday I collected a lot of money. I got quarters and cents and loonies and twonies and pennies and five cents.

Celebrating success	Markus, you are rich! Read your story to me and let me hear about all your money. You know the names of so many coins and you have been brave and used your sounds to tell me all about it. You have all the sounds for the words "money," "quarters" and "pennies." You really stretched the words. Good for you!
Extending the language	Tell me where you collected your money. What were you collecting for? Who helped you with your collection? Where do you keep all your money? Can you count it?
Extending the writing	Markus, you have told all about the pennies and nickels and quarters and loonies and twonies. I liked hearing about your money. What else could you tell in your story?
Setting a goal	When you write your story tomorrow, try to tell more about it. I would like to hear more of your ideas.

Identifying the Need

Students are ready to learn how to extend their thinking about their stories and to thereby write longer stories. They have learned a number of things about how to put down their ideas on paper. They are making good matches between sounds heard in words and letters they know. Although they still may not have control over spacing and punctuation, they are experimenting. Able to draw and tell about details in their oral stories, they show a readiness to include those details in their written stories.

Getting Ready

- Arrange to use chart paper and felt pens or chalkboard, chalk, and eraser.

Teaching the Lesson

1. Engage the class in a scenario like this: "Children, I am going to write a story for you. Watch me." Write a brief story, such as this:

   "Yesterday I got a new puppy." The end.

2. Prompt students to read the story with you. Ask them what they think of it and invite them to raise questions about the story.

3. In response to children's questions, and with their participation, add more sentences to the story. For this stage of writing development, two or three more sentences are enough. The story could develop like this:

   Yesterday I got a new puppy. It is small as a toaster. It is black and white. It has three white feet and one black foot.

4. Engage students in a discussion about changes you have made in the story and how they improve the story so the reader will enjoy hearing about the puppy. You might say something like this:

   "What do you think of the story now? Do you think our sentences make the story better? Why? Now we know a lot more about the puppy. We know what color it is, how big it is. Can you imagine the puppy with three white feet and one black foot? Can you visualize the puppy in your mind? That is what a good story can do. It helps us to visualize what it's describing."

5. Ask students to consider what they would like to write about and to share their topic ideas with a partner. They can further tell their partners two or three things about the chosen topic.

6. Call on students to give examples of topics and ideas. Help extend student thinking with questions such as these:

   - Where did this happen?
   - What did this look like?
   - How did it make you feel?
   - What was funny or unusual about what happened?

Building Criteria
• **Include details in your story.**

7. Tell students that you want to see if they can write more sentences than they ever have before. If they have been writing one sentence, then they might try to do two or three. Challenge the class: Who can write the longest story of their lives today? (Later, give the children who achieve a personal best a round of applause.)

Prompting Student Review

- Did you write more today than you did yesterday?
- What details did you include in your writing?
- What will you remember to do when you are writing?

Monitoring Student Progress

- Is the student able to write more today than before?
- Are the student's sentences connected and do they make sense?
- Does the student understand how to expand on a central idea?

Today I go to the gym. I sang S-A-N-T-A and Teddy Bear Song. When we go back we sang We wish you a merry Christmas!

Chapter Ten: Reinforcing the Learning—Writing Stories

Let's pause for a moment and give the children time to consolidate the mini-lessons they have had so far in Writing Workshop. Expectations are building for their writing development: they must write more, consider topics they want to write about, and make their pictures full of detail.

Complementing these mini-lessons in Writing Workshop are lessons in basic skills, offered at other times of the day. Students have been encouraged to use Elkonin boxes to stretch out their words to hear all the sounds. Phonetic spelling lessons have started and formal printing instruction has begun with students now expected to space their writing and to use lowercase letters only (capital letters are too easily misused).

As children are consolidating all the writing skills taught so far, the teacher is doing daily demonstrations that incorporate the lessons on story development and the basic skills lessons in areas such as printing and spelling.

The teacher selects topics from the shared experience of the class or from personal experience, noting aloud for students where the idea comes from and reiterating that their lives are full of stories. Finally, the teacher celebrates success. Each time a child is able to demonstrate application of the lessons taught so far, the teacher shows the class and celebrates what the writer can do. Nothing succeeds like success!

On the following pages are selected examples of the teacher working alongside students to give them the nudge they need to apply the lessons. On page 63 there is an example of a consolidation lesson in Writing Workshop, where the teacher models all the skills taught to date.

One day I made a car with my dad and me and I was surprised.

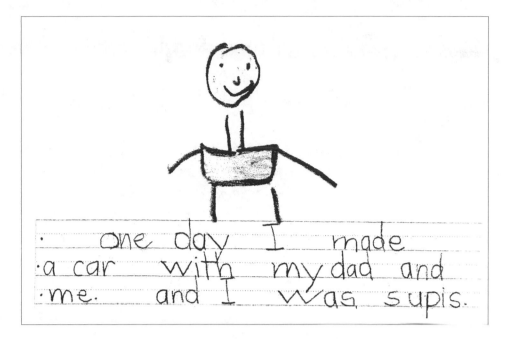

Celebrating success	Jaecen, I see you are printing on the lines and making your letters the correct sizes. Good for you and look at all the words you have written correctly!
Extending the language	Tell me about the car you made. What did you use? Which parts did you make? Which parts did your dad make?
Extending the writing	You had a lot of fun with your dad. What else can you add to your story to tell a little more about your car?
Setting a goal	You have so many good ideas. I would like you to write longer stories now. We have lots of time for writing and you need to fill your time with more story writing. Try to write a longer story tomorrow.

What's next? Building volume and fluency

My Mortimer and me went to go to bed and I kept on singing and I sang. I went downstairs and the policeman said, "Be quiet." Seventeen brothers and sisters said, "Be quiet, " and everyone fight and I went to sleep.

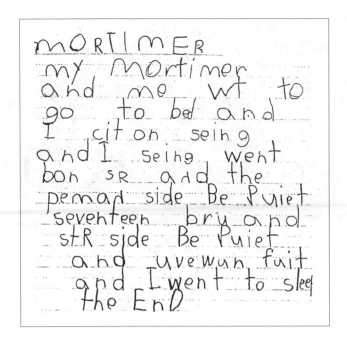

Celebrating success	Axel, you have written such a long story! I am so pleased with your long story today. Look how many sentences you have written.
Extending the language	Who else told Mortimer to be quiet? Has anything like that ever happened to you?
Extending the writing	You are doing very well with putting in lots of sounds in the words. Let's look at some of the words and practise stretching out the sounds and putting in some more letters.

Let's try the word "went." How many sounds do you hear?

w-e-n-t. That's right, there are four sounds. I will put four spaces here _ _ _ _ and let's put in all the sounds in order.

Now let's try the word "kept." How many sounds to you hear?

k-e-p-t. That's right, there are four sounds. I will put four spaces here _ _ _ _ and let's put in all the sounds in order.

Now let's try the word "sister." How many sounds do you hear?

s-i-s-t - r. That's right, there are five sounds but there are six letters. I will put five spaces here _ _ _ _ _ and let's put in all the sounds in order. I will show you that *er* on the end of a word is made with *e* and *r*. |
| **Setting a goal** | When you are writing your stories, say the words slowly to yourself. Stretch the word out so you can hear more of the sounds. Try to put in letters for all the sounds you hear. |

What's next? Representing more sounds with letters

Sample Consolidation Lesson

Time	Purpose	Writing Workshop Activity
4 minutes	Warm up.	The teacher engages students in a consideration of topics. "Let's think of something to write about today. Where will we get our idea? Oh, hot dog day. Sure, that's a good one. I need to visualize hot dog day so I can make a detailed picture."
6 minutes	Model putting details in the picture as rehearsal for writing.	The teacher talks out loud as she draws her picture. "I always buy two hot dogs. I open them up and put in ketchup and mustard. If I was at home I would put on pickle relish, onions and tomatoes. I like my hot dogs spicy. There in my picture you can see my two hot dogs with all the toppings. I like to sit beside my friends in the lunchroom. I will draw them in my picture too. Oh, and I mustn't forget my milk!"
2 minutes	Model printing on lined paper with spaces.	"I have my chart ready. I will put some dots down the side to show myself where to print so I don't get lost. I am going to count down two from the top and put a dot there. Then I will count down two and put a dot there." (And so forth.)
8 minutes	Model the writing process, stretching out sounds, making phonetic matches, and writing several sentences to tell the story behind the picture.	"What would be a good way to start writing about hot dog day?" Who can help me with the beginning sentence?" *I can smell the hot dogs.* "Let's see, I will use only lowercase letters for a while. I need to start by the dot. I—remember the space—can s-s-m-m-e-e-e-l-l-l the h-h-h-o-t d-o-g-s." (And so forth.)
40 minutes	Select topics and write.	"What would you like to write about today? Let's hear your ideas." (Students contribute topics. The teacher calls out a title for each one and students begin to write.)
5 minutes	Recap the lesson.	• Who found a story topic from their own life? • Who remembered to make a picture with lots of details? • Show your picture to a partner. Tell your partner about all the details you put in your picture. • Who was able to write lots of sentences? • Who remembered to put in the printing dots? • Who remembered to use lowercase letters? Show your partner the smart things you did with your sentences, your spacing and all your lowercase letters. • Give yourself a clap for your hard work today!

Chapter Eleven: Writing from Your Life

Yesterday night we played in bed. We each got a button phone and we got (our) own gun that makes a sound.

Celebrating success	Markus, let me tell you about all the great learning I see in your picture. You have put lots of details in your picture and used up all your white space. You have made such a long story and I see a period at the end. I can hardly wait to hear this story! Read it to me.
Extending the language	Playing in bed is such fun! Can you tell me about your beds? Are they bunk beds? Tell me about your brother. What other games do you like to play?
Extending the writing	I am so pleased that you did such a good job of stretching out the sounds in all these words. I can read this story easily. I also liked that you put spaces between your words! You are a fearless speller. Look at this hard word—*button*! You aren't afraid of hard words, are you? You did a great job of spelling this word!
Setting a goal	I like the way you told details about what you were playing. You even gave a detail about the gun—you said it makes a sound! Tomorrow you can write more stories about some of the other fun things you and your brother do. Don't forget to tell all the details!

Identifying the Need

The children have reached a level of confidence and fluency in their writing. They are ready to begin to craft their writing to the demands of a particular genre. In this case, it is personal writing, memoir, or, as we say to children, "True Stories from Your Lives." This lesson, and those that follow in Chapters 12 to 16, lead the children through the development of personal stories in a step-by-step manner. This first lesson encourages students to look for story-writing topics in their everyday lives. At the end of the lesson, students consider a new list of criteria for story writing. This new list will begin their understandings of creating true stories from their lives.

Getting Ready

- Assemble some stories on varied topics written by children in the class.
- Have a chart stand with paper and felt pen ready.

Teaching the Lesson

1. Tell students that they have come so far in their writing that they are now able to write true stories from their lives. Explain to them that *anything* can be a topic for a story: their walk to school, their thoughts in bed last night, the game they played with their brother, a caterpillar crawling on a leaf.

2. Read aloud a variety of stories from the children's writing books, and engage students in a discussion about story topics, as well as other things they can write about. Record answers, cluster them on a web such as the one on the next page, and then print them on a chart for referencing.

3. At the end of Writing Workshop, say to children, "We are going to discover how to write great stories from our lives. We have made a beginning by thinking about the things we might like to write about. I am going to start a new chart where we will build our criteria for these stories together."

4. Print at the top of a blank chart: What makes a great story from my life? Read the question aloud.

Building Criteria
- **Find a story in your life.**

5. Tell children that the first thing they need in Writing Workshop is to find a story that they think is interesting. Say something like this:

   "When you go home tonight, I want you to look for a story in your life. It might happen at the dinner table. It might happen when you are watching TV. It might happen at bedtime. Maybe it will happen in your dreams! Our lives are full of stories. Watch for one tonight, and remember it so you can write your story during Writing Workshop."

Our friend and colleague, Carrie Sleep, discussed topics for writing with her class. Carrie introduced the topic web and some children had ideas to contribute right away. Carrie returned to build the web at intervals throughout the first term as the children got more topic ideas from trade books and from stories written in the class. She also wrote her own stories on some topics that the children had not discovered. Her example Introduced them to new opportunities for writing. Here is an adaptation of the web from Carrie's class:

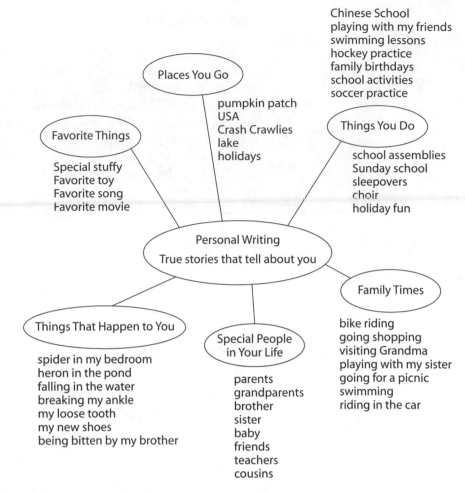

Places You Go
pumpkin patch
USA
Crash Crawlies
lake
holidays

Chinese School
playing with my friends
swimming lessons
hockey practice
family birthdays
school activities
soccer practice

Things You Do
school assemblies
Sunday school
sleepovers
choir
holiday fun

Favorite Things
Special stuffy
Favorite toy
Favorite song
Favorite movie

Personal Writing
True stories that tell about you

Things That Happen to You
spider in my bedroom
heron in the pond
falling in the water
breaking my ankle
my loose tooth
my new shoes
being bitten by my brother

Special People in Your Life
parents
grandparents
brother
sister
baby
friends
teachers
cousins

Family Times
bike riding
going shopping
visiting Grandma
playing with my sister
going for a picnic
swimming
riding in the car

Prompting Student Review

- Where do good writers look for things to write about?
- Where are you going to look for your story idea tonight?

Monitoring Student Progress

- Reflect on each student's contributions of story topic ideas. Is the student thinking more broadly or should you provide more encouragement to venture out into less familiar topics for stories?

Chapter Twelve: Starting with a Title

Holly is a leaf. Santa is real. I love Rudolf. I love Christmas. I love my Christmas tree. I love Christmas Eve.

Holly N a leaf,
Santa is real,
I love Roodoff.
I love Chistmas
I love my Chist
mas tree,
I love Chistmas
eve.

Celebrating success	Raymond, you have so many sentences! I can see that you are working hard. You can spell so many words and you are using capital and lowercase letters in the right places. Good for you!
Extending the language	Let's talk about your favorite part of Christmas. Tell me all about it. Why do you like it the best?
Extending the writing	Raymond, you have written about so many different things today: about holly, Santa, Rudolph, your Christmas tree . . . Perhaps, you could write a whole story about *just* Santa, or *just* the Christmas tree, and tell all about it.
Setting a goal	Tomorrow when you write, put a title at the top of your page. That will remind you to write lots of sentences about just one thing.

Identifying the Need

The volume of student writing indicates that the student is ready for further crafting of the content. One way to promote this is to establish a clear focus. Inclusion of a title is a signal to young writers. When children print their titles first, it focuses them on their topics. The title acts as a plan for their writing and helps them avoid the rambling, repetitive writing often seen in Grade 1. Fully developed personal writing expresses engagement with the topic.

Getting Ready

- Find samples of student work in which titles have been used.
- Choose about six story books that have been read aloud to the class.

Teaching the Lesson

1. Stand the story books up on the ledge so that students can see the covers. Discuss with students that stories have titles. Read the titles together and ask students what they notice about them. Students might say that titles appear in larger printing and that they are often placed in the middle of the page at the top.

2. Show students examples of how their classmates have used titles. You might say something like this: "Just like our story book authors, our friends are using titles too. Look at Queenie's story. She is writing about shopping with her mom. Queenie's title is 'Shopping with my Mom.'" Continue to highlight other examples in a similar manner.

3. Engage students in a discussion about what makes a good title. They might say that a good title is short, catches people's attention so they will want to read the story, and signals what the story will be about.

4. Ask the children to think of their topic for writing today. Invite them to share their ideas with a partner. This activity should take little more than five minutes.

5. Invite children to tell the class, gathered on the carpet, what their titles will be before they return to their seats to begin writing.

6. As students tell their titles, offer guidance in making them short and catchy, like this:

> Student: Me and my friends are going skating.
> Teacher: "Going Skating!"
> Student: We play tag at recess.
> Teacher: "Recess Fun."

If they choose, students may later change their topics and titles.

Although many children will have titles before they begin to draw or write at their seats, some children may need to spend some time drawing before they can come up with a title. A good rule of thumb for a child who cannot think of a writing topic is to ask him to start on a picture and think while he draws. Perhaps an idea will come while he is drawing!

On your class's evolving criteria chart, add this reminder: Start with a title. It will prompt students to focus their stories.

Prompting Student Review

- What makes a good title?

Monitoring Student Progress

- How many students were able to apply the mini-lesson today?
- Which students generated a catchy title that can be used for an example tomorrow?
- Who needs a reminder about writing with a title?

APRIL FOOL'S DAY

Today is April Fool's Day. I am going to do an April Fool's joke on my dad and it is going to be a good one. I am going to do a good April Fool's joke and I am going to put some ice cubes on his toe. I will play a joke on my mom. I am going to play a joke on my brother.

—by Darren

SKATING

Today I get to go to skating lessons again. I will get new skating shoes. They are white. I will put them on today. They are comfortable. They help me skate. We will be skating in the same place. My teacher is called Florence. She teaches lots of things. She is a good teacher. I know how to skate now. I was proud. I was very proud.

—by Melanie

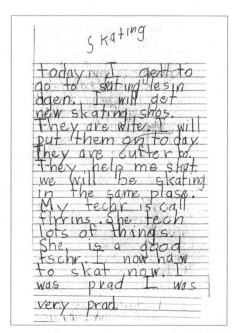

Chapter Thirteen: Making All the Sentences Belong

MY LITTLE SISTER

My little sister can be a monster because ..."Wait!" she shouts. Because she interrupts me. But I still love her! She is in preschool still. One of my sister's teachers had a baby! Today we are going to see the baby. Oh, did I mention it's a girl? My mom said maybe I could help them. She said that if my dad said yes. He said maybe. The baby's name is Alice, I think.

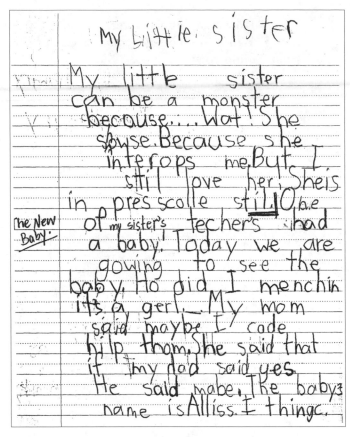

Celebrating success	Kaitlin, you have written quite a long story today. I think you're excited about going to see the baby.
Extending the language	Tell me some other monstrous things your sister does. Were you ever a monster when you were little? I think I was.
Extending the writing	The title of your story is "My Little Sister." Let's read your story again and see if it is all about your little sister. Whoops! I think you got so excited about this new baby that you forgot to make all your sentences match your title. I can see two stories here. You worked twice as hard today! One story is "My Little Sister." It stops at your word "still." What should be the title of the second story? *The New Baby.* That's a good idea. Let's write "The New Baby" here. You wrote two stories today!
Setting a goal	Tomorrow I am going to give the class a lesson about making all the sentences match the title. See if you can try that idea in your writing tomorrow.

Identifying the Need

As students are learning to tell about a personal moment or incident from their lives, they need to remember to make sure that they focus only on that moment or incident and do not go off topic. This lesson encourages students to check their work to make sure that all sentences belong. It builds on teaching students to start with a title.

Getting Ready

- From the writing students did in the last Workshop, choose samples that feature titles.
- Prepare a demo story on the chalkboard or on chart paper.

Teaching the Lesson

1. Show the student samples that have titles. Highlight those that are short, catchy, and well matched with the content of the story.

2. Reveal the title of the demo story you have written for students and ask students what they think the story could be about. Here is an example:

Falling into the Pond

Yesterday my husband was cleaning the goldfish pond in the garden. He fell into the pond. He came in the house and changed his clothes. He went outside and he worked in the garden. He mowed the lawn. He was busy all day in the garden.

3. Read the story with the class, and then ask them which sentences tell about falling into the pond. Read the sentences one by one and ask the students, "Does this sentence tell about falling into the pond? Does this?" Put a line through all the sentences that do not relate to the title.

4. Invite students to suggest ideas for other sentences to replace the ones that do not fit well.

5. With student suggestions, rewrite the story. For example, you might get something like this:

Falling into the Pond

Yesterday my husband was cleaning the goldfish pond in the garden. He was walking along the tippy rocks on the side of the pond. A rock tipped and he fell into the pond! He was muddy and wet. His shirt was dripping, his hair was dripping. He was wet all over. He said, "I think I scared the fish."

6. Again, ask students to judge whether each sentence tells about falling into the pond. Explain to students, "The title is a signal for the reader and for the writer. It tells what the story will be about. The writer must make sure that all the sentences belong to the title."

As you circulate, draw the attention of the class to examples of students' titles and how they catch your interest. Let students know that you are looking forward to reading stories with such interesting titles!

Building Criteria
• **Make all sentences belong.**

7. Tell students that before they leave the carpet area to return to their seats, they need to consider their topics and share their titles in partners. Remind them that the title goes at the top in the middle as a signal for the writing. They must try to make all the sentences belong.

Prompting Student Review

• What do good writers do to let readers know what the story will be about?
• What are some of the titles you used in your writing today?
• Do all of your sentences belong with your title? Check each one.

Monitoring Student Progress

• Was the student able to write with a focus on one incident or event?
• Did the story relate to the title?
• Did the story contain relevant details to make it interesting?

You may need to follow up this lesson on subsequent days by writing more stories on the board and asking students to identify sentences that "don't belong." Also, read aloud student samples that stay with the topic to provide models for the class.

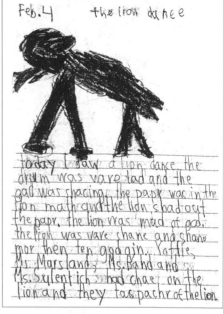

One day I had a garage sale. I made enough money to buy a Gameboy. We sold old toys like Duplo, trains, cars, some videos, baby toys, an old bike and other old stuff. People came from all over town to buy stuff like trains, cars, Duplo and videos. We had it in the summer.

—by Cameron

Today I saw a lion dance. The drum was very loud and the ground was shaking. The paper was in the lion's mouth and the lion spit out the paper. The lion was made of gold. The lion was very shiny and shined more than ten gold coins. Yoffie, Ms. Marsland, Ms. Bahd, and Ms. Sulentich had a try on the lion and they took pictures of the lion.

Chapter Fourteen: Remembering Details

MY MOM'S BIRTHDAY

It was my mom's birthday. We had a good time. We had fun. We ate lots of good food. We enjoyed the food. We had cereal for breakfast. Salmon for lunch and for dinner we had pasta.

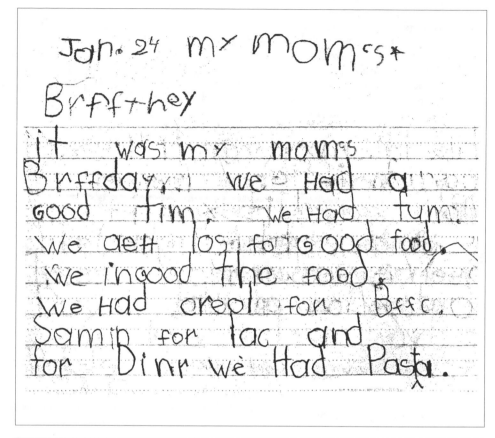

Celebrating success	Jennifer, you remembered to start with a title. Well done! I can see you were very brave in sounding out hard words like *enjoyed* and *salmon*. I can tell you had lots to eat at your mom's birthday.
Extending the language	Tell me about your favorite meal. Help me to taste all the parts you enjoyed so much. Tell me how it looked on the plate so I can get the picture in my mind.
Extending the writing	You have told me all about the pasta dinner. You said it was spaghetti with tomato sauce and meatballs. You put grated cheese on top. The meatballs were so big you could eat only one! Now I can imagine the birthday dinner. Your words make me hungry! You told me lots of details.
Setting a goal	Next time you write, it will help you if you close your eyes and imagine just what it was like in that place at that time and tell all about it. Try to make your reader see it just the way it was.

When reinforcing this lesson during storytime read-alouds, consider the author Ezra Jack Keats. Ezra Jack Keats demonstrates adding details to small events. In his book, *The Snowy Day*, the story revolves around a few moments outside in the snow. In *Amy's Letters* whole pages are written during the moments a letter is caught in a gust of wind while Peter chases it. These are excellent book choices to illustrate how authors use this strategy.

Identifying the Need

This lesson is best taught when students are just beginning to elaborate on aspects of their personal stories. They have some volume in their work and feel confident about crafting their writing, which, of course, will be enriched by the addition of personal details.

Getting Ready

- Prepare a demo story on a topic that is familiar to the students, but forms a list rather than an in-depth description of a single event.

Teaching the Lesson

1. Show students how to stretch a moment to add detail. Begin by reading together your list-like demo story.

   ### At the Park

   > I went to the park with my dad. I went on the swing. I went on the slide. I went on the monkey bars and I played in the sand. I had fun at the park.

2. Lead students to realize that all the sentences are about the park, but that the story is a *list*. Tell them that a better story would be to take one of the ideas and say more about it. "We could use a magnifying glass and look carefully at just one of the things I did at the park. Which one will we try?"

3. With role play and imagination, lead children to explore one of the topics in detail, perhaps, "I went on the swing." After asking the students to close their eyes, visualize, and think about what they are doing on their swing, prompt them to say some of their ideas out loud. Quickly record their ideas on the board to create a story that might go something like this:

   > I went on the swing. I sat in the seat and held onto the cold chains tightly. I called to my dad, "I want to go high! Please give me a big push!" My dad pushed me HARD and I went up and up until the chain bounced. "Higher!" I called.

4. Engage students in comparing the two stories. Ask questions such as these:
   - Which story helps us to see the experience at the park?
   - Which story has more details?
   - Which story is more fun to read?
   - Which story is more fun to listen to?

5. Prompt students to picture in their minds what they are writing about today. Prompt them to see where they are, to observe what is happening around them, and to think of the details. Ask them to close their eyes and remember every detail.

6. Ask students to tell their partners about the "tiny" moment they thought about and encourage them to tell the whole thing.

7. Before sending students to write, remind them to think about the steps for writing a story with details.

Step 1: Think of something interesting that happened to you.
Step 2: Make a picture in your head.
Step 3: Think about all the actions in the order they happened.
Step 4: Write all about it so the reader can see the time with you.

Building Criteria
• **Remember to answer Who? Where? How? What? Remembering details will help stretch a small event into a story.**

Prompting Student Review

• Tell me what good writers do to make an interesting story.
• Did you try to stretch out a moment so that readers could see it in their minds?
• Which parts did you find easy? hard?
• What will you remember for next time?

Monitoring Student Progress

• Would the student's work serve as a demonstration piece tomorrow?
• Does the student need more coaching with this lesson?

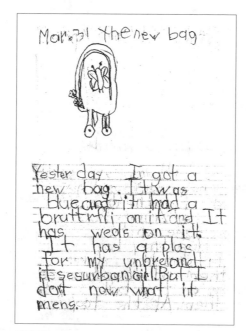

THE NEW BAG

Yesterday I got a new bag. It was blue and it had a butterfly on it. It has wheels on it! It has a place for my umbrella and it says, "Urban Girl" but I don't know what it means.

—by Jennifer

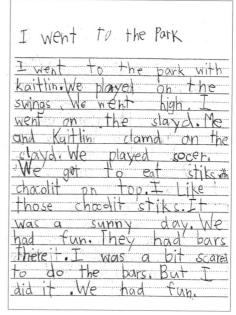

I WENT TO THE PARK

I went to the park with Kaitlin. We played on the swings. We went high. I went on the slide. Me and Kaitlin climbed on the slide. We played soccer. We got to eat sticks with chocolate on top. I like those chocolate sticks. It was a sunny day. We had fun. They had bars there. I was a bit scared to do the bars, but I did it. We had fun.

—by Yotti

Chapter Fifteen: Adding Direct Speech

THE BROKEN PIPES

On Saturday I helped my dad dig the big hole because our pipes are broken. We dug a big, big big hole. And then we put the new pipes in the hole. Also we put a big white bucket with two medium holes for the pipes to go through. Then the water from the kitchen will go all the way down to the white bucket.

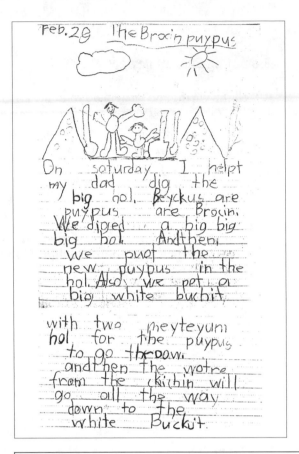

Celebrating success	Markus, this is a long and interesting story! You really explained all about the hole and the pipes. You have started with a title and you have included a lot of details. Well done!
Extending the language	Which part of this job was the most fun for you? Tell me all about it. What were you thinking? What were you and your dad saying to each other?
Extending the writing	Sometimes, including talking or thinking in a story helps it to come to life. You can put a speech bubble in your picture to show what you were saying to your dad.
Setting a goal	Tomorrow when you write your story, you could write exactly what the people are saying and then put bubbles around those words.

Identifying the Need

Students are ready for this lesson when they have lots of volume in their writing and confidently choose topics and stretch personal experiences to include more detail. When they learn how to add talking or thinking it makes their stories come alive and strengthens the sense of voice.

Getting Ready

- Find examples of cartoon strips in which characters speak or think in bubbles.

Teaching the Lesson

1. Show students how writers use speech or thinking bubbles with the cartoon strip examples. Point out the difference between talking and thinking bubbles for characters.

2. Tell students that good writers use speech to make the story come to life. Draw a picture and write a scene from a familiar story without the well-known dialogue (see the sample text below). Ask students what they notice.

   > Papa, Mama, and Baby Bear came into the kitchen. They noticed that part of their porridge was gone. They were surprised and angry. They started to look for the person who had eaten their porridge.

3. Engage the children in conversation, asking, "What is missing from this story? What do you think of the story written in this way? How can we make the story come to life?"

4. As children identify that direct speech is missing, ask them to tell you what each of the characters said. Write their thoughts above the characters' heads and then add bubbles. Your conversation might sound like this:

   "What did the Papa Bear say when he saw that his porridge was gone? That's right. 'SOMEONE'S BEEN EATING MY PORRIDGE!' I am going to write that above his head. Then I can put a speech bubble around it just like they do in the cartoons. It's easier for me to add the bubble after I've written what Papa Bear said."

   And so forth.

5. Rewrite the scene to include the direct speech. As you write, show students the quotation marks that go around the words first enclosed in speech bubbles.

6. Explain to students:

   "When we read the scene from the Three Bears I put on the board, it wasn't any fun. The story didn't come to life. When you write your stories, you can make them come to life if you put in some talking too, but not too much! Just one sentence to make it more interesting for us to read. Try it with your story today."

It may be a while before students can apply the punctuation skill of going from speech bubbles to quotation marks, but some students will understand right away and it is worth introducing at this point.

Building Criteria
- **Use talking to make your story come alive.**

Prompting Student Review

- How many of you were able to include talking or thinking bubbles in your picture and story today?
- Turn to a partner and show your partner what you said in your story.
- Why is it a good idea to include talking in a story?

Monitoring Student Progress

- Would bringing forward the student's work help my teaching tomorrow?
- Does the student need more help to apply this lesson?

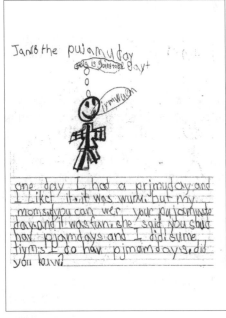

PAJAMA DAY

One day I had a pajama day and I liked it. It was warm but my mom said, "You can wear your pajamas today" and it was fun. She said, "You should have pajama days," and I did! Sometimes I do have pajama days. Did you know?

—by Cameron

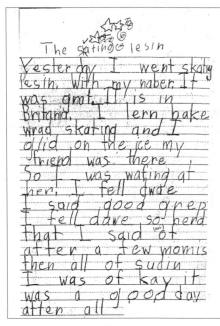

THE SKATING LESSON

Yesterday I went skating for a lesson with my neighbour. It was great. It is in Britannia. I learned backward skating and I glided on the ice. My friend was there so I was waving at her! I fell down. I said, "Good grief." I fell down so hard that I said, "Ouf!" After a few moments then all of a sudden I was okay. It was a good day after all.

—by Melanie

Chapter Sixteen: Expressing Your Feelings

[THE CARD GAME]

One day I played cards with my sister Jessica. The game was called Crazy Eights. We halved the cards. I picked up a ten and my sister picked up an ace. My sister got to go first. Because the ace is the highest card. My sister won the first game. Then I won the second game.

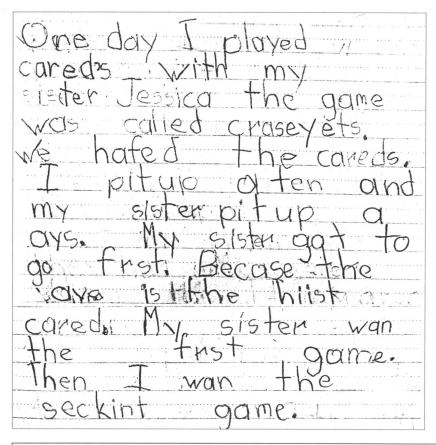

Celebrating success	Jennifer, you started with a title and you made all your sentences belong to the card game. Well done! You used your sounds for all those hard words too. Look, I see *highest* and *second*. You made good matches with those words.
Extending the language	I like to play Crazy Eights too. My children could always beat me at that game! They would be so happy. I wished I could win sometimes. You are lucky. You and your sister had a tie! How did you feel when you tied the second game? I bet you were proud of yourself.
Extending the writing	When authors show us how they are feeling in a story, we can enjoy it more. What could you add to your story to tell us how you felt? Yes, let's write: "I felt proud of myself." That would be a great addition to your story.
Setting a goal	Tomorrow when you write, think about telling your feelings about what is happening in the story. You could say I was excited or I felt sad. Sometimes we can just put in an exclamation mark and that shows the reader how we are feeling too. See what you can do with that idea tomorrow.

Identifying the Need

If many students are writing short, stilted sentences, it would be a good time to introduce them to the idea of writing with emotion. Doing this will expand sentences and add life to the work.

Stories come alive when readers become of aware of character's feelings as well as their actions. Emotion gives writing its voice and individuality. It can be added in the picture in words, and by punctuation. Even one sentence with an exclamation point can make a piece of writing much more personal and alive.

Getting Ready

- Choose about six student-written stories in which emotion is implied, but not stated explicitly.
- Write two demonstration stories on the board or on chart paper. You might use those by Chantal and Kaitlin.

Teaching the Lesson

1. Engage the children in a discussion of all the things they know how to do in story writing. Refer to the class's evolving criteria chart. Then advise them: "Today you will learn another way to make your stories even better. Today you will learn about expressing your feelings in stories."

2. Choose several stories from classmates to read aloud. Use expression in your voice to demonstrate emotions implied in the writing. Ask the students to tell you how they would be feeling if the same thing happened to them. Discuss possible emotions for each piece of writing.

3. Read aloud and discuss each of the following student samples or select two from your own class in which feelings are expressed vividly.

MY DAD

My Dad is on an airplane. He is going to go to Vietnam. He is maybe going to come back at April or May. I miss my dad. I wish he is coming back now! I wish, I wish, I wish. He went on Sunday. My dad was not happy to go there. He told me that he is not happy. I like my dad. I said, "Good bye," before he left and I kissed him before he left. Then I've been sad for a few days.

—by Chantal

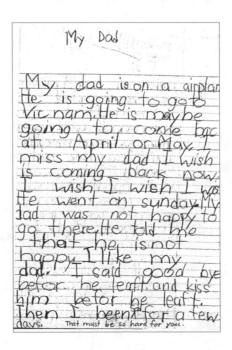

a) Engage students in a discussion of how Chantal showed her emotions. It might sound like this: "How was Chantal feeling in the story? How can you tell? What did she do to show us?" Possible answers include

- repeating "I wish"
- saying "I miss my dad. I wish he is coming back now!"
- using exclamation marks
- saying that she has been sad

MY GRANDMA

Tomorrow my grandma is going to pick me up! My grandma is picking me up because my mom's dad, "Po Po" is going to a funeral because my Auntie Anny died. When they are gone we are going to do art, stories, games, maybe park. My grandma is the best. If someone wanted to do a trade I'd say, "NO!!" She's my grandma! I love her! I love her!

—by Kaitlin

b) Engage students in a discussion of how Kaitlin showed her emotions. It might sound like this: "How was Kaitlin feeling in the story? How can you tell? What did she do to show us?" Possible answers include

- repeating "I love her!"
- saying, "If someone wanted to do a trade I'd say 'No!'"
- using exclamation marks

4. Ask students to watch for chances to show their emotions in their stories. Remind them that they can use punctuation, dialogue, or sentences to show the reader just how they are feeling. You and your students may want to generate a chart listing words for feelings, such as *happy* and *sad*.

5. As students are writing, stop them and prompt them to talk to their partners about the feelings expressed in their stories. Ask them to show the ways they will include feelings in their writing.

Building Criteria
- **Show your feelings. Use talking, !, or feeling words, or show the reader how you are feeling through actions.**

Prompting Student Review

Tell me about the feelings in your writing today.
- Who used talking to show feelings? What did you say?
- Who used an exclamation mark?
- Who said something like I felt sad, I felt happy?
- Who showed their feelings in a different way?

Monitoring Student Progress

- Should I use this student sample to celebrate success tomorrow?
- Can the student express emotions through writing?
- Does the student need more help with this?

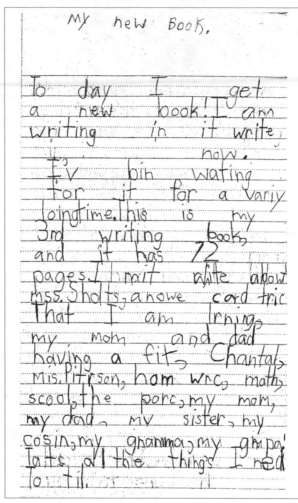

MY NEW BOOK

Today I get a new book! I am writing in it right now. I've been waiting for it for a very long time. This is my third writing book and it has 72 pages. I might write about Mrs. Schultz, a new card trick that I am learning, my mom and dad having a fight, Chantal, Ms Petersen, homework, math, school, the park, my mom, my dad, my sister, my cousin, my grandma, my grandpa! That's all the things I need to tell.

—by Kaitlin

Chapter Seventeen: Reinforcing the Learning—Writing Personal Stories

It is a strategic time to pause and give children an opportunity to consolidate the mini-lessons they have had so far in Writing Workshop. They now have a list of criteria to help them shape their personal narratives more powerfully. Classes have been taught five dimensions of writing craft, summarized below, and once they have consolidated this learning, they will move on to fictional narrative.

What makes a great story from your life?

1. *Start with a title to focus your story.*

2. *Ensure that all sentences belong.* Write only about your topic.

3. *Stretch a moment with details.* Make a picture in your head or on a four-square paper. Think about all the things that happened. Help the reader to see it with you.

4. *Use talking to make your story come alive.* Start with talking and thinking bubbles in your picture.

5. *Show your feelings.* Use talking, !, feeling words, and action described in sentences to show the reader how you are feeling.

Complementing these mini-lessons in Writing Workshop have been lessons in conventions, offered at other times of the day. Students have been encouraged to spell high-frequency words correctly and to use capital letters and periods appropriately. They have been introduced to exclamation marks as a tool to show emotion in their stories. Phonetic spelling lessons and formal printing instruction are continuing.

As children are consolidating all the writing skills taught so far, the teacher is doing daily mini-lessons that reinforce these skills. The teacher also does daily demonstrations of story development, reviewing all the criteria for personal narrative, and of ways to apply the lessons taught about conventions.

The teacher selects topics from the shared experience of the class or from personal experience, noting aloud for students where an idea comes from and reiterating that their lives are full of stories.

Finally, the teacher celebrates success. Each time a child is able to apply the lessons taught so far, the teacher shows the class and celebrates what the writer can do. Nothing succeeds like success!

On the following pages are examples of the teacher working alongside students to give them the nudge they need to apply mini-lessons. On page 88, there is an example of a day in Writing Workshop, where the teacher models all the skills taught to date.

Yesterday I went to Science World.
I saw a real tarantula. It was hairy.
I saw a stickbug too. Its arm was
very sticky. I saw a man holding
an snake. Me and my brother
petted it.

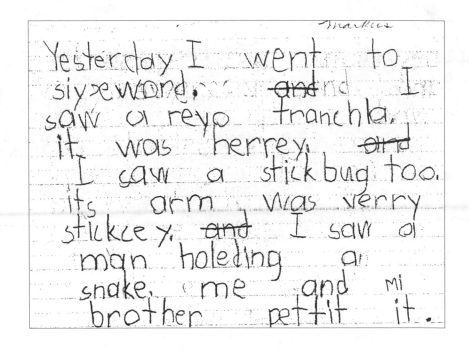

Celebrating success	Markus, you do such interesting things with your family. You always have ideas for your writing. Oh, you are brave to pet a snake and touch a stickbug. I enjoyed your story.
Extending the language	Tell me more about the snake. I'd love to hear about it.
Extending the writing	I notice in your writing today you put the periods in the right places, but then you started the next sentence with the word "and." Remember the rule about *and*. Let's go back in your story together and cross off the ands.
Setting a goal	Remember, when you put a period at the end of the sentence, the reader gets to take a breath. Start the next sentence with a capital letter but no *and*.

What's next? Avoiding *and*

AIR HOCKEY

Yesterday me and my brother played air hockey. I won my brother lost. We played on a table. There was a switch on the ground. It was for the air. The puck was red. There was a net for scoring. You can play bowling, or chess, or cards. You can play any games you like.

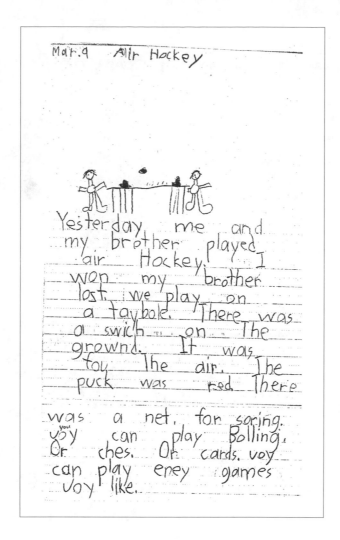

Celebrating success	Markus, you must have fun with that air hockey game. You included a lot of detail in your story. There are lots of games you can play on it.
Extending the language	Tell me what strategy you use to beat your brother at hockey. Is it as much fun as playing hockey at the rink?
Extending the writing	I see that you are brave and using your sounds to figure out lots of the words. That's great. But there are some words you should always remember now. One of them is YOU. Y-O-U. You know that one. Let's spell it together. Now look at your story. How did you spell it here? Yes, it's backwards. Let's go back in your story and fix every *you* together.
Setting a goal	Remember that this is a word you need to write correctly all the time. If you forget how, you can check the list of words at the front of your writing book.

What's next? Spelling high-frequency words correctly

MY DAD

I love my dad. He is the best. He plays games with me. He loves me all the time. He helps me fix my games. My dad takes me to my soccer practice. He takes me home. I really like my dad.

Celebrating success	Shiv, I love your story. It touches my heart. You have really shown why you love your dad. You gave lots of details in your story. I can tell your dad spends lots of time with you and cares for you.
Extending the language	What kind of games do you and your dad enjoy playing together?
Extending the writing	Shiv, you have put most of the periods in just the right places. Well done! Do you remember what we need to do after a period? That's right! Start with a capital letter. Let's go back in your story together and put them in.
Setting a goal	When you are writing tomorrow, remember what comes after every period. A capital!

What's next? Practising capital letters and periods

We made gingerbread cookies today. On Friday we get to eat it. I hope my gingerbread girl will not run away from me. When it comes out of the oven I hope it will not run away.

Celebrating success	Jessica, you have done a beautiful job today. I like your picture of our gingerbread people. Your story makes me laugh. Wouldn't it be funny if our gingerbread people ran away?
Extending the language	What would that gingerbread girl say if she ran away? What would you say?
Extending the writing	I notice that you have some extra capital letters in your writing today. Remember we are trying not to use capital letters for a while. Capitals are too tricky for us right now. Let's go back in your story and change those capital letters together. I will help you.
Setting a goal	When you do your writing tomorrow, try to remember to use lowercase letters.

What's next? Losing unnecessary capital letters

Sample Consolidation Lesson

Time	Purpose	Writing Workshop Activity
10 minutes	Warm up.	Children join with the teacher, Ulla, in reading favorite poems about spring on charts. Ulla asks, "Do you enjoy spring too? You might like to write about the parts of spring you enjoy in your writing book today."
10 minutes	Demonstrate use of a basic skill with a story.	"I have written a story on the board for you. It's a true story from my life. It happened on the weekend. Take a look at it. What do you think of my story? The following story without appears *without* any punctuation: I felt the warm spring air on my cheek. I had an idea. "Ahhh, what a perfect day for a bike ride!" I said to myself. I quickly got the key and opened the door of the shed. There it was, my old blue bike. What a sorry sight! It was covered with cobwebs, the tires were flat and the chain was squeaking. "Time for a tune-up," I thought. I got out the wrench, the pump and the oil. An hour later we were on the road, my bike and I. Ulla, who showed students the use of punctuation marks earlier during shared reading, guided reading, and read-aloud sessions, engages them in a discussion of the punctuation needed in the story. The class reads and rereads the story to insert appropriate punctuation and capital letters.
5 minutes	Discuss criteria.	Ulla asks children to look at the class's criteria chart and see if her story contains all the criteria they have learned for personal narrative. Title? All sentences belong? Details? Talking? Feelings? She reminds them to include these things in their writing today. She reminds them to focus for the whole writing time.
5 minutes	Celebrate success.	Ulla reads stories that represent personal breakthroughs for students. They include examples of spelling high-frequency words correctly, adopting the personal writing criteria, and writing in greater volume.
45minutes	Discuss topics and write.	Ulla asks, "What will you write about today? Think about these two things: What will my title be? What feelings did I have in this story? Tell your neighbor. Now raise your hand to tell all the class and then start writing."
10 minutes	Share the writing.	Students meet each other on the carpet and read each other's stories. They do simple editing as they are able.
5 minutes	Debrief.	Ulla asks: • How many of you looked at the criteria chart and checked to see if your writing had all the parts it needs? • Did you check for capitals and periods in your writing today? • How did you help yourself to focus on your writing today? The children respond to the last question in this way: • I just kept on writing and writing. • I had a good idea. • I didn't talk to my friends. • I moved to a quiet place in the room. • I tried my spellings myself. • I skipped the picture and started writing right away. • I tried to fill the whole page. The Workshop ends with applause.

Chapter Eighteen: Introducing Story Grammar

One day Kitty and Kit liked books. Their room was messy—not with socks, toys, clothes and food, but their room was filled with books. They loved reading books. Kitty and Kit read ten books a day. There were books under their beds, in the sink, in the dressers and stacks on the couch. They have pictures about books and albums about books. Kitty ordered books. Kit bought books.

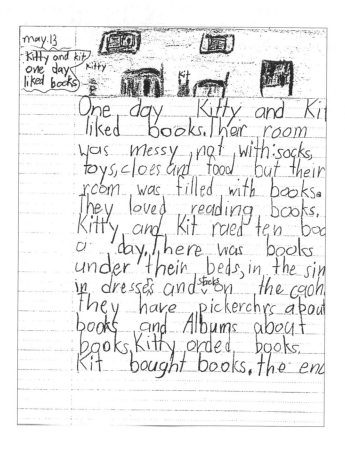

Celebrating success	Crystal, you have used story language to help me see the room full of books. You have set up the problem so beautifully in your story. I love the part where you said, "There were books under their beds, in the sink, in the dresser and stacks on the chairs." Well done.
Extending the language	What are Kitty and Kit going to do about all those books? How will they solve their problem? Tell me about it.
Extending the writing	You know we've talked about how many stories have problems and solutions. Tomorrow when you come back to your writing, you could write about how Kit and Kitty will solve the problem of the books. That will make your writing even more interesting.
Setting a goal	Your story gives me an idea. I need to teach the class about how the problems in stories need to have solutions. Your story has a great problem. Would it be OK with you if I use your story to teach the class about problems and solutions?

Identifying the Need

Before this lesson is taught, students are taught the elements of story grammar during read-alouds and in reading groups. Students have had many opportunities to review the elements of story orally, in guided lessons or with a partner. They are familiar with story structure before being asked to demonstrate this knowledge in writing.

Understanding the narrative form happens over a period of years in many small increments. In Kindergarten, teachers ask, "What happened at the beginning? the middle? the end? Which character did you like best? What is your favorite part?" In Grade 1, the conversation around narrative continues with more in-depth discussion of story elements. It may take only a few repetitions for students to identify the components of a story, but it may be years before they are able to use all the components to write one well. Narrative is a complex and demanding form that requires lessons over several months and many demonstrations.

This lesson is best taught when children's spontaneous writing reveals an interest in story writing and children have consolidated many of the skills taught in personal narrative. With fictional narrative, it is especially important to watch for the teachable moment. As an example, one year a student named Steven wrote a story about Hoppy the Rabbit. The teacher, Ulla, invited Steven and the rest of the class to write more stories about Hoppy, and soon students were writing about Hoppy in space, at the pyramids, in the school play, and more.

Getting Ready

- Choose a story with a well-defined story grammar for reading aloud. Any of Leo Lionni's well-known books, such as *Swimmy* and *Frederick*, have well-defined story grammars.
- Photocopy, enlarge, and post the story grammar map blackline master (page 114) or write an outline on the chalkboard or white board.
- On Retelling a Story, a blackline master (see page 115), paste some illustrations of key events in the story in the left-hand boxes, or draw some of your own. Enlarge the page to legal or 11 × 17 size, one copy for each student.

Teaching the Lesson

1. Read the story aloud, pausing to ask students for their input in completing the story grammar map. It might sound like this: "Who are the people in this story? The main people are called the characters. Let's write their names here on the story map. What is the problem the characters have? Where will I write about the problem?" And so on.

2. Tell students to tell the story they have just heard to their partners, using the ideas listed on the story grammar map. Guide this process effectively by saying thinks like, "Partner A, tell Partner B about the problem in the story. On our chart, we have written some reminders." (Read aloud what is on the chart.) "Partner B tell Partner A about what the characters did to resolve the problem."

3. Hand out photocopied sheets and tell students to write the story with the pictures to guide them. Emphasize that since they know the story, the story will be long! Encourage them to use all the space on their paper, to look at the story grammar map to remember the parts, and to "tell the whole thing!"

Prompting Student Review

- Show me in your story where you have talked about the characters, the problems, the events, and the ending.
- Did you write a long story?
- Did you tell all the important parts of the story?

Monitoring Student Progress

- Was the student able to improve the volume of written work by writing a known story?
- Was the student able to incorporate the elements of story grammar into the retold story?

Once upon a time there was a prince and a princess and an evil witch. They were married and they had a baby. One day when everyone in the kingdom was asleep an evil witch took their baby and in the morning the baby was gone. "Call the guards!" shouted the mom. "My baby's gone. Call the knights. My baby is gone!"

"We will find your baby for you. I bet it is at the haunted castle. The baby must be in the dungeon. Ask one person, but only one."

"Okay, let's go but let's go to a farmer."

He gave them a unicorn and the unicorn was fast. They got there and fought the witch. She died and the baby was grown up and they got back safely.

Celebrating success	Elizabeth, what a great story! You have a problem, some characters, and some action. Your setting is in a castle and a dungeon. Well done!
Extending the language	I like the story language that you used. It sounds like a fairy tale. You said, "Call the guards." Tell me some other story language you used in your writing. It really makes it lively.
Extending the writing	I would like to use your story to show other children how to start a story and create an interesting problem. I can really see how upset the mother is! At the end, do you think you could tell more about what happened when they got to the witch?
Setting a goal	Remember that you need to give some details at the end of the story too. I like the way you told what happened at the beginning with three or four details. Tomorrow, when you get to the end of the story, remember to add some details.

Story Grammar

Title
Author
Setting
Character
Problem
Events
Solution

Identifying the Need

Once students are familiar and comfortable with story grammar, it is time to teach this lesson. Students will understand the meaning of all story elements, and have heard and analyzed these elements using story grammar. They will be building on experiences working with the whole class, working with partners, and having teacher demonstrations.

It is very common in our experience that young children's stories end abruptly. They appear to exhaust their interest and their ideas and just want the story to end. Celebrate the inventiveness and volume of work done. If your writers are capable, fluent writers, you might suggest returning to develop the ending a bit more another day. Don't press this point too hard, though. Children at this age often think the story is "just fine" the way it is.

Getting Ready

- Enlarge a copy of the story grammar blackline master (page 116) or outline story grammar on the board.
- Obtain large pieces of chart paper and felt pens for each pair of students.
- Decide on working pairs for the writing activity.

Teaching the Lesson

1. Share examples of students' spontaneous story writing or refer to Elizabeth's story on the first page of this chapter. You might say:

   "Listen to Elizabeth's story. See if she has all the parts to her story. Listen and see who are the characters? What is the setting? What is the problem? How did it get solved? Remember. These are all elements of what we call story grammar."

2. Invite students to use the story grammar outline to build a story with you. It might sound like this:

   "You know all about the parts of a story. When I read a story to you, you can take it apart, and tell me each of the pieces of the story. Today we are going to do that backwards! We are going to imagine all the pieces and then put the story together!

   "Let's start with the characters. Who will be the people in our story? Will they be human or animals? What will their names be?

   "Let's think about the setting for our story. Where do you want our story to take place?

   "Okay, now we have our characters and our setting. What problem could these characters have in this place?

   "Now we need to know what the characters are going to do about the problem. How can they solve it? Who might help them?

   "How will our story end? Will it be a sad ending with the problem not solved or a happy ending with a solution to the problem?

   "Who can think of a good title for our story? Let's think of more than one title. Who has another one?"

   As you question the students, fill in the elements of the story grammar.

3. Engage students in telling the story from the plan: "Let's tell our story out loud using our story grammar. Listen, and I will get us started. Then you can help me." Say a sentence or two and then ask various students to contribute a sentence or two each, pointing at the chart as they make their way through the story.

4. Prompt the students to write the story with partners.

"How will your story start? Will you say once upon a time? Will you say one day in [describe the setting]? You will need to talk to your partner about how you will begin. Then use the ideas from our story grammar to put the pieces of the story together. I am excited to see all your story ideas. We will come back and share them at the end of our writing time."

Children will need guidance about sharing the work and the writing. Perhaps they can each write a sentence. The student who is not writing can help spell and sound out the words.

Prompting Student Review

- What are the parts of a story?
- Meet with another pair of writers and trade stories. Read each other's work and talk about the parts you like best.

Monitoring Student Progress

- Was the student able to use the story grammar to develop a story?
- Will the student need more practice with this? Or, is the student ready to use the story grammar to plan stories independently?

WHEN RABBIT MET KATY

It was the first day of Kindergarten and Rabbit had no best friends and so did Katy. Their teacher, Ms. Lilly, made up a game that needed partners. Every body had their best friend as a partner but Rabbit didn't have one. So Ms. Lilly put Rabbit with Katy. At recess Ms. Lilly was outside watching the kids. Katy was playing with some of her new friends and asked Rabbit if she wanted to play. Rabbit nodded. After recess it was centres time at centres. Rabbit asked Katy if she wanted to play house with her. Katy said, "Yes." Soon it was home time and that's how they became best friends.

—by Cathy

Chapter Twenty: Shaping a Story into a Poem

SPRING

I love spring! Spring has my birthday, spring has flowers, spring has me. Spring is wonderful! Spring has butterflies, spring has animals, spring has birds to sing. Spring oh spring, what a nice time in spring.

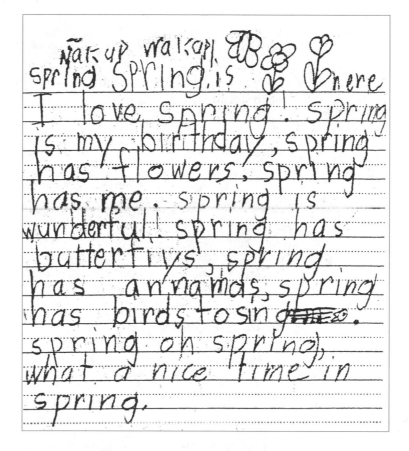

Celebrating success	Melanie, this writing is just like a poem. It makes me think of spring and sunny days. I can see pictures in my mind of butterflies and flowers. Your writing makes me feel happy.
Extending the language	You have used the word "nice." I think your writing would be more interesting to the reader if you used a more powerful word. Let's think of some together: *beautiful, lovely, happy, great*. Let's try each one in the sentence and see how it sounds the best. Which is your favorite?
Extending the writing	You have written in the shape of a story today, but your ideas sound just like a poem. If you want to change this story into a poem, you would need to make some changes in the sentences. Poets like to have short lines and long lines and they use white space to give the poem a shape. I will teach the class how to turn a story into a poem. May I use your story to teach the class?
Setting a goal	When you write stories that show lots of feelings, like this one does, you can turn them into poems by changing the shape. Let's try that next.

Identifying the Need

The best time to teach this lesson is when spontaneous student writing demonstrates that children are experimenting with poetry-like ideas, such as repetition of a word beginning each sentence, imagery that uses the words "like" or "as if," and sensory details. Children will have had a fair amount of exposure to poems through read-alouds and their own reading. Group writing of poems, where the teacher scribes ideas and "powerful language" on a particular subject in the shape of a poem, will also have happened throughout the year. By this time, students have mastered many conventions and criteria for personal writing. They will enjoy expanding their options for writing and can likely succeed with the poem form.

Getting Ready

- Select a sample of student writing that expresses "poetic ideas" but is written in story form, or use the example on page 95.
- Write the sample on a large chart or make an overhead transparency and display it where all the children can see it.
- Have felt pens and chart paper nearby.
- Gather a selection of poetry books to demonstrate poem shapes.

Teaching the Lesson

1. Read the sample several times together. Draw students' attention to the aspects of the writing that make it seem poetic:

   - repetition
   - language use
   - sentiments
   - imagery

   Melanie's story about spring has these features.

2. Explain to children that writing that has these elements can be written like a poem. Tell them, too, that a poem has a different shape than a story.

3. Display the books of poetry and ask students what they notice about poem shapes. They will likely make these observations:

   - The lines in a poem do not stretch across the page like a story.
   - Some lines are long, others short.
   - Some poems are shaped like a cloud or a fish.

4. Engage children in changing the story by their classmate, or the example provided, into the shape of a poem. Use an alternate color of felt pen to draw the line breaks on the transparency or chart paper. For example:

   Spring

   I love spring! // Spring has // my birthday, // spring has // flowers, // spring has me. // Spring is wonderful! // Spring has // butterflies, // spring has // animals, // spring has birds to sing. // Spring oh spring, // what a happy time in // spring.

Spring

I love spring!

Spring has
      my birthday!

Spring has
      flowers!
Spring has me!
Spring is wonderful!
Spring has
      butterflies.

Spring has
      animals.
Spring has birds to sing.
Spring, oh spring,
What a happy time
      in spring.

Write the new lines on a fresh chart or overhead as you go. The discussion might sound like this:

> *"Where do you think we should break the first line of this poem? Why would that be a good spot? Look, as I write it again on the chart.*

> *"What should we write in the next line? Look, I can move this line in. That way I can make my poem shape even more interesting. Notice every time I start a new sentence I begin with a capital letter. That is one thing most poets do.*

> *"Now what should we write? Yes, we're making a pattern. We're writing "Spring has" on one line and then telling what it has on the next line. People will enjoy reading a poem in this shape."*

And so forth.

5. Invite students to write a poem. Since poems often have a lot of feeling in them, suggest that they think of something they really enjoy—their writing will flow more easily. Encourage them to set their poems into a shape, just as the class did with the sample. If students have shared an experience, it might be worthwhile to create a web together to generate ideas and images. Below is an example Ulla used with her Grade 1 class after they had spent a week learning to rollerskate. All of the students then wrote poems.

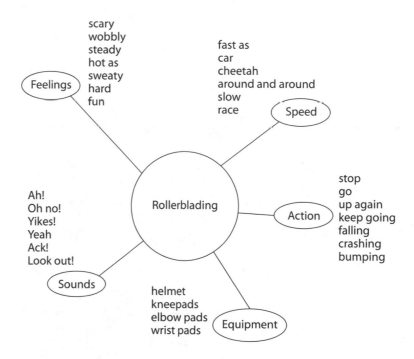

Building Criteria
• **A poem has a shape.**

Prompting Student Review

• Who tried to write a poem today? Let's see your poem's shape.
• Read the favorite line of your poem out loud to the class.
• Why is that a good line for a poem?

- Can I use the student's writing for celebration tomorrow?
- Did the student show risk taking by trying a poem form?

ROLLERBLADING

I put on my helmet
I put on my knee pads
I put on my elbow pads
I put on my wrist pads
It's Rollerblading
time.
Hey, I'm doing it.
I'm going, going
I'm steady, steady
I'm wobbly, wobbly
I crash!!
Ouch! My bump hurts.
I'm going, I'm going
I'm zooming
    I'm zooming
Yes I passed Yotti
Boom! I crash on the wall.

    —by Tony

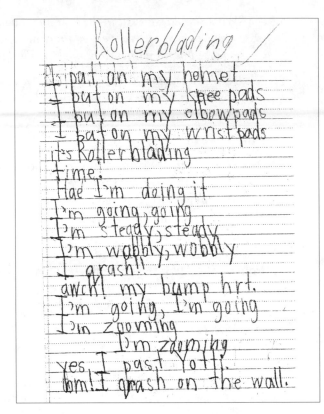

MY DAD

My Dad
just
    came
back.
    He
bought
us
two pair of shoes.

He bought
toys
he brought
lots of
things. The best
things he
brought was love.
I love my dad!

    —by Chantal

RED

Red is Santa Claus's suit.
Red is a valentine's heart
that makes sad people into happy
people.
Red is an apple that grows on
trees.
Red is a cherry that birds take.
Red is a robin that flies
so high. Good-bye.

—by Shiv

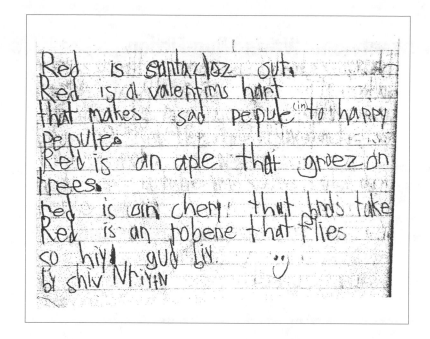

MY FISH

My fish
is
crazy. My fish
swims that way →
My
fish
swims
this way ←

My fish swims
everywhere. My fish swims
that way → My fish
swims this way ←
My
fish
swims
up up up and
down down down!

—by Kaitlin

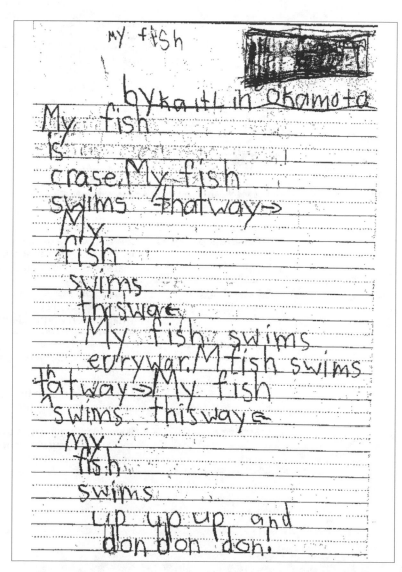

Chapter Twenty-one: Writing Non-Fiction

PLANTS

Plants can grow in different ways. There are many types of plants like strawberries, rose trees, sunflowers and daisies. Plants have roots, stems, leaves and some have petals. Some plants have nectar and branches.

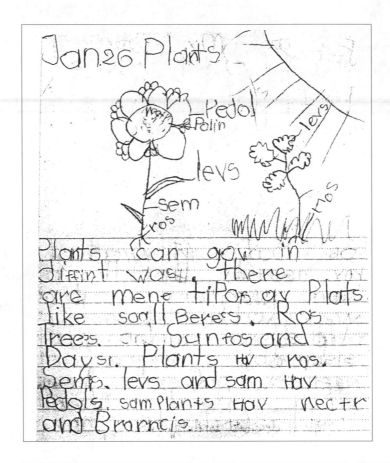

Celebrating success	Jennifer, what a great idea! You have written about our science lesson. You know all about plants. You have a labeled diagram that shows about your story.
Extending the language	I see in your picture you have labeled the sun, the water, and so many parts of the plant. What does a plant need? Do you know what the parts of the plant do?
Extending the writing	I notice you haven't used the words "water" and "sun" in your story. What could you say about water and the sun and the plants? I would like to teach the class about non-fiction writing. May I use your plant story to show them a good way to do it?
Setting a goal	It would be a good idea to do another diagram tomorrow and try to use all your words in sentences. I'll look forward to your new non-fiction story.

Identifying the Need

When spontaneous student writing reflects an interest in non-fiction topics, it is time to introduce non-fiction writing. Having demonstrated competence with the writing criteria taught to date, students can now begin to understand and enjoy this important writing form. Units taught in Science or Social Studies provide interesting content. This lesson helps expand writing across the curriculum.

Getting Ready

- Assemble samples of labeled diagrams students have done in content-area studies.
- Assemble non-fiction books that contain labeled diagrams and that children are familiar with. These might include any books by Gail Gibbons, Scholastic's Go Facts series, or Nelson's PM Non-Fiction series.

Teaching the Lesson

1. Explain to the children that you are going to teach them another form of writing, one called non-fiction. Explain that non-fiction books tell important facts about real things. In non-fiction, authors can "teach" about something they know, perhaps starting with a "teaching picture." Using an example of student writing that is similar to Jennifer's example from the previous page, or Jennifer's sample, you might say:

   "Look at the picture Jennifer has made today. She has a flower, a plant, and the sun and it's very pretty, but Jennifer's picture is not just a pretty picture. It is a teaching picture. What do you think helps us to learn when we look at her picture? Yes, that's right. It has labels all over it to show the important parts of the plant."

2. Read Jennifer's writing, or an equivalent by one of your students, aloud. Help children to notice that the student used most of her labels in sentences to tell true facts about plants.

3. Explain to students that a labeled diagram is a great place to begin non-fiction writing. You may want to stop the lesson here and encourage children to make a labeled diagram and write on a non-fiction topic today.

4. Tell students that another way to develop non-fiction writing is by making a web and basing writing on it. Develop a web with students. The key words in the web can come from students' background knowledge or from text they are reading. If using text, read it sentence by sentence and ask, "What is one important word that we could write on our web? Where should I put it?"

5. Choose one section of the web to demonstrate non-fiction writing. For example, consider "Dogs: Look like," from the web on the next page. Think aloud to model the process for students and write down your non-fiction sample.

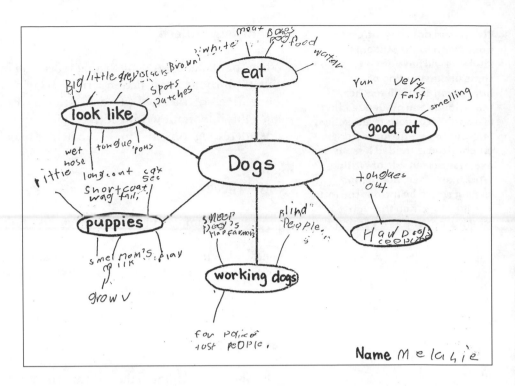

Name Melanie

Building Criteria
- Draw and label a picture or make a web.
- Use all the important words in sentences.

We prepare students for non-fiction writing in reading groups and literature studies outside of Writing Workshop. In subject areas such as Science and Social Studies, students write from webs and make labeled diagrams with guidance from the teacher. When students are familiar with this genre, we introduce it into Writing Workshop and ask students to use these forms as they write about subjects that personally interest them.

Teacher says	Teacher writes
I need to write my title.	Dogs
The key words are big and little. I will start with those.	Dogs can be big or little. Dogs can be black, brown, grey or white. Their coats can have patches or spots. A dog's tongue sometimes hangs out and its nose is supposed to be wet. A dog's feet are called paws.
I see words for the colors of dogs too.	
Now I can write about their coats. I am going to write it just beside my sentence about the colors.	
I need to write about their wet noses, their tongues and their paws. What will I say? Where will I write it?	
Have I used all the key words about what dogs look like? Great! . . .	

6. Encourage children to try webbing or labeled diagrams and to use their key words in sentences to teach about something they know. Once again, ask them to think of a topic that appeals to them and share their initial ideas with a partner before developing a web or drawing.

Prompting Student Review

- What non-fiction topics did you choose to write about today?
- Show your partner the web you made.
- Did you remember to use all your key words in your sentences?
- Read your most interesting true sentence to your partner.

Melanie's piece of non-fiction writing grew out of her web, shown on page 102.

Monitoring Student Progress

- To what extent are students able to use the labeled diagram or webbing strategy to generate their own non-fiction ideas?
- To what extent are students able to develop key words into sentences?
- What else are they ready to learn about non-fiction writing?

DOGS

Dogs are all kinds of sizes. Some dogs are small. Some dogs are big. Some dogs have spots and patches. They have wet noses. They have pink tongues. Dogs have sharp paws. They eat meat. Mostly they eat biscuits. They like to chew bones. They drink a lot of water. They run very fast. Dogs stick their tongues out to keep cool. Sheep dogs help farmers. Some dogs help blind people. Some dogs help police find lost people.

—by Melanie

VEHICLES IN THE AIR

There are many vehicles that can fly in the air. The first one is called helicopters. Helicopters do not need a runway when they take off. They can go straight up. The second one is called jet planes. The biggest jet plane is called the Jumbo Jet. The Jumbo can carry 500 people. The third one is called blimps. Blimps have cabins under their balloons. The fourth one is called seaplanes. Seaplanes land in the water. Seaplanes do not have wheels.

— by Markus

Following the modeling done by the teacher in the Dogs unit, Markus read a story about flying vehicles, developed a web independently and went on to write this non-fiction piece. When teachers demonstrate ways that children can capture and shape their ideas for writing, the students gain even greater control.

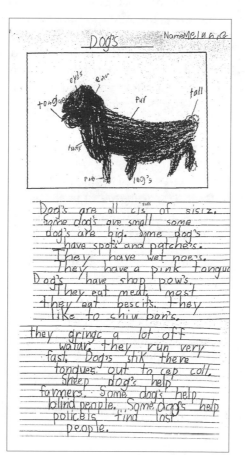

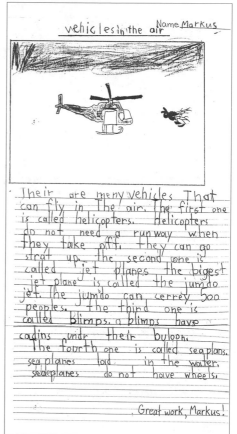

Chapter Twenty-two: Reinforcing the Learning—Reviewing Genres

The children have now had exposure, instruction, and guided practice not only in personal narrative, but in the fictional narrative, poetry, and non-fiction genres. They have many options available to them in Writing Workshop and can turn to criteria to guide them in the various forms of writing.

The teacher continues to provide demonstrations and modeling so that children can learn to use story grammar independently to plan and write stories. She reinforces these understandings:

- Stories have characters—people or animals.
- Stories have settings where the action takes place, such as a farm, a castle, a jungle, or outer space.
- Stories are based on a problem or problems that characters have to deal with.
- Stories have a structure of beginning, middle, and end, which follows the characters from learning about the problem to trying to solve it, to succeeding in solving it.

These ideas can be summarized and displayed on a criteria chart.

In mini-lessons about poetry, the teacher emphasizes these concepts:

- *Shape:* A poem has a different shape than a story. It may have long lines, short lines, or lines of even length.
- *Feelings:* A poem often shows how the writer feels.
- *Repetition:* A poem often has lines that repeat.
- *Images:* A poem makes a picture in your mind.

These can be reinforced and presented on a criteria chart.

In mini-lessons about writing non-fiction, the teacher emphasizes these understandings:

- Make a labeled diagram. Use the words from the labeled diagram to write your facts in sentences.
- Make a web. Use the words from the web to write your facts in sentences. Be sure to use all the words from the web.
- Start with an opening sentence that will catch the reader's attention.
- Use text features in non-fiction. Use boldface words, headings and subheadings, a glossary, and a table of contents.

These practical ideas could also serve as the basis for a criteria chart in the class.

We find this Writing Workshop stage one of the most satisfying. We are delighted by the spontaneity, richness, and variety of writing that invite our response. Children, too, are pleased with the range of choices available to them and express pride in their abilities to manage topic and form with confidence.

From here, young writers continue to experiment with the four genres at their disposal, selecting both form and topic. The teacher continues to work alongside them, celebrating, encouraging, and watching for trends in the class that indicate children are ready for another refinement in form or style.

The following at-the-elbow conferences show how the teacher might reinforce and encourage students to apply the skills taught in the various genre studies.

MY TEACHER

I have
A teacher. Her name is
Ms. Petersen
She is the one who
Teaches us.
She changes
Our seats.
She lets us
Play at recess. I
Love our teacher.

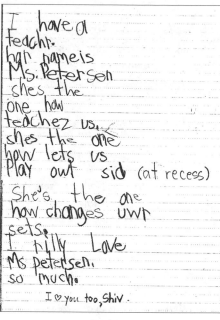

Original   Revision

Celebrating success	Shiv, you have written several poems about someone you care about. It is such a good topic for a poem. You wrote a poem about your little brother, your baby cousin, and today you wrote about me! I'm so happy. Let's read it together and hear how it sounds.
Extending the language	You said, "She is the one who teaches us." So, what are some of the things I teach you? These are good details that you can include in your poem.
Extending the writing	I'm thinking about repetition. I really like the words "she is the one who . . ." How would it sound if you repeat that part in the next line? That's right. She is the one who changes our seats. Where else could we repeat that? I'll just write the words on the side, and if you want, tomorrow you can write the poem again with that repetition.
Setting a goal	Next time you write a poem remember to read each line out loud as you write so you can hear how it sounds. Remember that a poem often has a pattern or a part that repeats.

What's next? Using poetic devices to make a better poem

THE NIGHT I FOLLOWED THE CAT

Every morning my cat Lindaly ran into the door like a plane. One early morning I woke up early to see what he is doing in the night. I saw him come out of a strange looking car. That night I decided to follow my cat. I rode my bicycle. The car went really fast so it's hard to keep up with him. Finally the car stopped. I followed him into a strange part of the town that I never saw before. I followed him into a building. I saw a door. There is a sign that says, Secret Scientist room. I opened the door. The light was off so I turn it on. There is my cat and a . . . rocket that had a super engine! Now, I remembered it's my birthday.

Celebrating success	I see you wrote a story much like the one we read together (*The Night I Followed the Dog* by Nina Laden). It's a good idea to take a favorite story and write it in your own way. I like the way you changed the ending. What a surprise to see what the cat was really doing at night!
Extending the language	What was the problem in the story? You wondered what your cat was doing in the night. In the end you found out, so the problem was solved.
Extending the writing	You wrote that you turned on the light and saw a rocket with a super engine. What was the cat doing there? Oh, he was building the rocket for you. And why did you just remember it was your birthday? Now I understand it better. How clever of you!
Setting a goal	When you write a story, remember to write everything that happened to make sure the reader understands. You can check by getting a friend to read it and see if he's confused. Then you know you have to explain something more carefully.

What's Next? Making the story make sense to the reader

SPIDERS

There are many kinds of spiders. I am going to tell you about trapdoor spiders. Trapdoor spiders have doors. If an ant comes near it the door will open and the spider will get it. Trap door spiders can eat wood bugs, and ants and crickets.

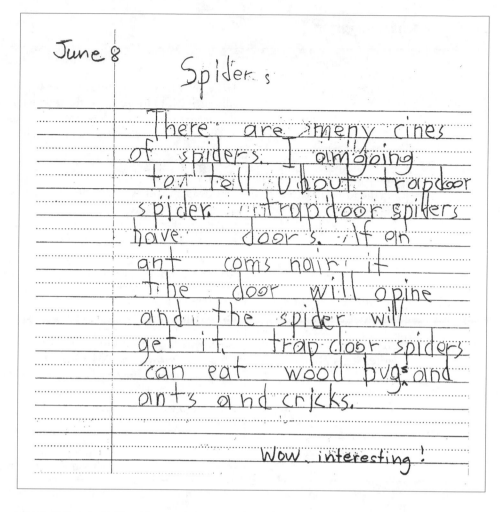

Celebrating success	Markus, you know so much about spiders and insects. How did you learn about the trapdoor spider? Oh, you read about it in Jennifer's book. What I really found interesting is when you say: "If an ant comes near it the door will open and the spider will get it."
Extending the language	What else does the book tell you about trapdoor spiders? Do they make webs? Do they live around here?
Extending the writing	Remember how we have learned to make a web of important facts before we write about a non-fiction topic. It's hard to remember all those facts in your head, and we want to know ALL about the trapdoor spider.
Setting a goal	When you write non-fiction, remember to tell as much information as you can. Next time you write non-fiction, you might start with a web.

What's Next? Adding more information to non-fiction writing

Sample Consolidation Lesson

Time	Purpose	Writing Workshop Activity
5 minutes	Provide a warm-up.	To begin her lesson on furthering an awareness of different forms of writing, Ulla elicits from the students the following forms to which they have been introduced: personal narrative, poetry, fictional narrative, and non-fiction. She briefly reviews the characteristics of each as they are identified.
10 minutes	Do a demonstration lesson, where children identify the form of writing.	Ulla puts Cameron's writing on an overhead, reads it out loud, and invites the children to identify what form of writing he has demonstrated. Many children quickly identify it as non-fiction, as it has lots of information about wolves, drawn from a big web posted in the classroom. Some children say the writing is a poem, though, because Cameron used a familiar poetic structure: "If I were … I'd …" They also notice the repetition of the word "I'd," also poetic. Ulla concludes that good writing can have poetic parts and non-fiction parts together. Authors make decisions about their own writing.
4 minutes	Provide further examples.	Ulla reads one or two pieces of writing that represent different genres of writing. She asks the students to identify the form of writing.
33 minutes	Students select topics and write.	She invites the students to think about their writing topics for the day. "Who has an idea for writing today? Remember you have many choices for writing. What's happening in your life? What are you really interested in? Do you have an idea for a story or poem?" Once all students have shared their topics and gone off to write, Ulla circulates, prompting and providing support and encouragement.
5 minutes	Share the writing.	Students who finish at about the same time meet on the carpet to read one another's stories out loud. They question or make suggestions, as they are able.
4 minutes	Recap the lesson.	Ulla surveys the class with these questions: • Who wrote on a non-fiction topic today? • Who wrote a poem today? • Who made up a fiction story today? • Who wrote a true story today? She tells the students, "You are such good writers. I love reading your writing every day."

June 1
2005

If I Were a Wolf

If I were a wolf i'd be a carnavor. I'd hunt for food. I'd hunt rabbits, mooses, beaver, fish, mice, deer, elk, caribou and buffalo. I'd have canines. I'd have thick fur in black, white, brown and gray. I'd have a long bushy tail and big paws. Long legs and a big long nose. Strong bones and big ears. Sharp teeth and 42 teeth. I'd hawl all night. I'd live in big wild places and have a huge territorie. But I'd- I'd - I'd - I'd -I'd be hunted.

Wow! Great writing!

i kn rit

I can write!

Information for parents and teachers about the early stages of writing development

Do you ever wonder why teachers seldom correct spelling and punctuation in young children's writing?

Teachers understand that just as children experiment with speech, delighting their parents with "mama" and "dada," so they must experiment with written language. When the child begins to scribble on paper, the teacher knows that with continued encouragement, instruction, modeling and practice, the child will develop writing skills.

Compare it to learning to ride a bike. No parents ever bought a bike expecting their child to win the Tour de France. The child needs time to practise, first, with training wheels to gain confidence and control, and later, with a parent supporting the bike, running alongside shouting words of encouragement. Eventually, all the skills will come together and the child will ride freely!

8.

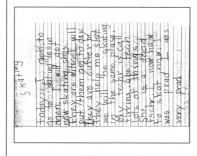

The teacher listens as he reads aloud and praises him for starting with a title and explaining his experience in detail. She praises him for risk taking, expression and knowledge of how to spell so many words. She will continue to teach him to make his writing expressive and refine his use of spelling conventions.

9.

Most conventions are in place now. The writing is clear and expressive. This child is ready to experiment with new forms of writing — story, poetry, and non-fiction. The training wheels are off, and the writer is ready for new challenges.

6.

The teacher says, "Read your story to me." She watches as he reads and points to the words. He says, "Yesterday, I collected a lot of money. I got quarters and cents and loonies and twonies and pennies and five cents." She praises him for trying so many sounds and for using some words he knows. She encourages him to write more sentences.

7.

Now the child's story is expanding, the printing is spaced, and the spelling is developing. The teacher listens as he reads aloud and praises him for writing a longer story and for applying the spelling lessons taught in class. She encourages him to start with a title and make all his sentences belong.

So it is with children's writing. Early scribbles give way to pictures, random letters become symbols for sounds and words, and sentences emerge with spacing, correct spelling and punctuation. All children pass through the stages illustrated below at varying rates, refining their efforts at each step.

To ensure that children are bold and confident learners, parents and teachers "run along beside" them, giving instruction, encouraging, and demonstrating. Too much correction early in the learning process will inhibit risk taking and undermine confidence. Risking errors leads to growth and greater learning in writing, just as in bike riding.

Here is how writing develops when children are given the pencil and instilled with the belief that they are writers.

1.

The child scribbles and writes his name. The teacher says , "Look at all your colors. Tell me a story about your picture. You are a writer!" Instruction follows in how to hold the pencil, where to place the picture, how to make the pictures colorful and representative.

2.

The teacher instructs the class in adding details to their pictures so that the picture tells a story. The teacher says, "Look at the details you put in your picture. I see you playing with your brother. You have started to make a picture that tells a story. Tell me your story."

3.

Now the teacher urges the class to write, saying, "Put in some letters you know. Use your favorite letters! Look, there is the alphabet. Pretend you can write!" The child finds words and prints letters he knows. The teacher praises his efforts. The teacher continues to instruct the class in sound-letter matches and begins to urge the children to apply these in their writing.

4.

The teacher says, "Tell me about your story." When the child relates that there is a flower and sunshine and a house, the teacher says, "Flower. What sound does flower start with? What letter makes that sound? Print it here." And so forth.

5.

Instruction continues in making sound-letter matches and stretching out the words to hear the sounds. The child is now able to represent more words with letters and to hear more than one sound in a word. The teacher says to the child, "Point to the letters in your story." She watches as he reads and points. He says, "I'm giving the duck food." She says, "Way to go!"

*The underscores indicate the sound-letter matches as the teacher transcribes the writing for her records.

Tips for Teaching ESL Learners About Writing

Although English as a Second Language (ESL) learners thrive when taught explicitly in Writing Workshop, it is possible to make specific suggestions for helping them.

- Have ESL learners engage in partner talk, not only about what they want to write about, but also about the process of writing: what will be done first, second, and third.
- Provide ESL students with appropriate sentence frames to help them respond to a question asked. By giving them a "frame," for example, "You would like to . . ." "I am going to play . . ." or "I wonder if . . .," you teach the language of response and also enable them to share their thoughts even when language proficiency is low. (Be cautious, though, as overuse of frames can make children dependent on them and their writing stilted and repetitive.)
- Look over the content of stories before you read them aloud. Introduce new vocabulary with sensory detail, drama, and artifacts. For example, if your story is about penguins in Antarctica, you might lead students in guided imagery where you pretend to dig in the ground and find it too hard because it is frozen, shiver, and demonstrate "frozen" through ice cubes.
- Use visuals when teaching and giving instructions always.
- Don't assume that all children understand a lesson. Many ESL students have difficulty because they are confused about basic vocabulary, such as *beginning, last, the one in the middle, below, above, the one before, after.*
- Teach school language: common nouns for direction and spatial awareness words. These can be enjoyable lessons for everyone and will give you insight into language comprehension across the class.
- Make as many activities hands on as possible. For example, give directions like these: Put your finger where you will start to write; show me where you will start a capital letter; if you hear one sound, put one finger in the air. The more a student has to demonstrate understanding, the more incentive there is to listen attentively and the more information you will have to monitor understanding.
- Use story retellings and drama often as devices for understanding.
- Provide a word bank for writing on a particular theme or subject. This word bank will remind students of the particulars involved in the pre-writing discussion.
- Before ESL students start to write, go to them and have short one-to-one conferences on what they will write about, helping them to frame their thoughts into coherent sentences.
- Remember that students find it helpful to know that past tense verbs usually have *ed* on the end and that *ing* words often need a helper like *is* or *was.*
- Encourage students in multiple ways: verbally, as in "Yes, that's good!"; non-verbally, as in nodding or smiling; and co-verbally, where your tone of voice conveys meaning and emotion.

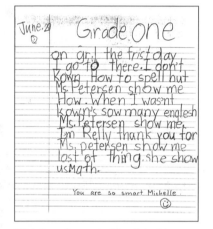

With just one year of English, this recent emigrant from China demonstrates ease in expressing her ideas in writing.

Story Grammar Map

Story Grammar Map of _____

Characters	Setting

Problem

Main Events	Solution

Note: For student use, enlarging to 11 × 17 size is recommended.

Retelling a Story

Title: _____

Story Grammar

Title

(What is the name of the story?)

Author

(Who wrote the story?)

Setting

(Where did the story happen?)

Characters

(Who is in the story?)

Problem

(What is it?)

Events

(What happened?)

Solution

(How did the characters solve the problem?)

Our Favorite Books for Children

Bloom, Becky. *Wolf!*
Browne, Anthony. *Willy the Dreamer.*
Browne, Anthony. *Willy and Hugh.*
Browne, Anthony. *My Dad.*

De Beer, Hans. *Ahoy There, Little Polar Bear.*
De Groat, Diane. *Roses Are Pink, Your Feet Really Stink.*

Fernandes, Eugenie. *A Difficult Day.*
Fox, Mem. *Hattie and the Fox.*

Gilman, Phoebe. *Something from Nothing.*
Gordon, Maria. *Dogs Can't Read.*

Hesse, Karen. *Come On, Rain!*
Hissey, Jane. *Ruff.*
Hughes, Shirley. *Dogger.*
Hutchins, Pat. *The Surprise Party.*

Kovalski, Maryann. *Omar on Ice.*

Laden, Nina. *The Night I Followed the Dog.*
Lionni, Leo. "The Alphabet Tree," from the anthology *Frederick's Fables.*
Littledale, Freya. *The Magic Fish.*
Lobel, Arnold. *Frog and Toad.*
Luenn, Nancy. *Mother Earth.*

Munsch, Robert. *Mortimer.*

Ryder, Joanne. *Lizard in the Sun.*
Ryder, Joanne. *The Snail's Spell.*

Sendak, Maurice. *Chicken Soup with Rice.*
Shannon, David. *No, David!*
Shannon, David. *A Duck on a Bike.*
Sheldon, Dyan. *The Whale's Song.*
Stewart, Paul. *The Birthday Present.*

Velthuijs, Max. *Frog Finds a Friend.*

Wishinsky, Frieda. *Oonga Boonga.*

Yolen, Jane. *Owl Moon.*

References

Applebee, Arthur. *The Child's Concept of Story*. Chicago: University of Chicago Press, 1978.

Bettelheim, Bruno. *The Uses of Enchantment*. New York: Knopf, 1976.

Buis, Kellie. *Writing Every Day*. Markham, ON: Pembroke Publishers, 2004.

Calkins, Lucy McCormick. *Nuts and Bolts of Teaching Writing*. Portsmouth, NH: Heinemann, 2003.

Calkins, Lucy McCormick, and Shelley Harwayne. *Living Between the Lines*. Portsmouth, NH: Heinemann, 2001.

Chapman, Marilyn L. *Weaving Webs of Meaning: Writing in the Elementary School*. Toronto: ITP Nelson, 1997.

Clay, Marie. *Observation Survey*. New Zealand: Heinemann, 1993.

Cunningham, Patricia M., and Dorothy P. Hall. *Making Words: Multi-Level, Hands-on Developmentally Appropriate Spelling and Phonics Activities, Grades 1–3*. Torrance, CA: Good Apple, 1994.

Egan, Kieran. *Primary Understanding: Education in Early Childhood*. New York: Routledge, 1988.

Fletcher, Ralph, and JoAnn Portalupi. *Craft Lessons: Teaching Writing K–3*. Portland, ME: Stenhouse Publishers, 1998.

Fletcher, Ralph, and JoAnn Portalupi. *Writing Workshop: The Essential Guide*. Portsmouth, NH: Heinemann, 2001.

Graves, Donald. *Writing: Teachers and Children at Work*. Portsmouth, NH: Heinemann, 1983.

Harste, Jerome C., Kathy Short, and Carolyn Burke. *Creating Classrooms for Authors: The Reading–Writing Connection*. Portsmouth, NH: Heinemann, 1988.

Harwayne, Shelley. *Lasting Impressions: Weaving Literature into the Writing Workshop*. Portsmouth, NH: Heinemann, 1992.

McCarrie, Andrea, Gay Su Pinnell, and Irene C. Fountas. *Interactive Writing*. Portsmouth, NH: Heinemann, 2000.

Murray, Donald. *Expecting the Unexpected: Teaching Myself and Others to Read and Write*. Portsmouth, NH: Boynton Cook, 1989.

Portalupi, JoAnn, and Ralph Fletcher. *Nonfiction Craft Lessons*. Portland, ME: Stenhouse Publishers, 2001.

Routman, Regie. *Invitations: Changing as Teachers and Learners K–12*. Portsmouth, NH: Heinemann, 1991.

Routman, Regie. *Kids' Poems: Teaching First Graders to Love Writing Poetry*. New York: Scholastic, 2000.

Schultze, Betty, and Janine Reid. *Writers Alive for Grade One*. Vancouver: Vancouver School Board, 2004.

Smith, Frank. *Writing and the Writer*. London: Heinemann, 1982.

Stead, Tony. *Is That a Fact? Teaching Non-Fiction Writing K–3*. Portland, ME: Stenhouse, 2002.

Wells, Jan. *Literacy in the Kindergarten*. Vancouver: Vancouver School Board, 2002.

Wells, Jan, and Janine Reid. *Writing Anchors*. Markham, ON: Pembroke Publishers, 2004.

Index

Acknowledge effort, 12
Actual developmental level, 12
Adding direct speech, 76–78
Anxiety, 12, 13
Assessment, 22–23
Author's chair, 11
Avoiding *and*, 84

Big, bold, bright (3 Bs), 32
Breakthroughs, 11–12
Bridging strategy, 38

Children's books, 117
Class participation, 24
Conference, 22
    At-the-elbow, 20, 22, 24, 42, 46, 104
    One-to-one, 5, 111
Consolidating/consolidation, 12, 60, 83
    Sample lesson, 50, 63, 88, 108
Conventions, 35, 83, 96
Criteria charts, 21–22, 68, 80, 104

Demonstration/modeling, 12, 24, 32, 35, 50, 55, 60, 63,
    77, 83, 88, 93, 96, 104, 108
Detailed expression, 9
Developing criteria, 21–22
Developmental continuum, 18–19, 22–23
Direct speech, 76–78
Disequalibria, 12
Drawing, 15–16, 32, 35, 41, 44, 46, 55, 68, 77, 102

Elkonin boxes, 29, 60
Emotion, 79–82, 83
English as a second language (ESL), 111
Enlargements, 52, 90
Equilibrium, 12
Expressing your feelings, 79–82

Finding words and letters around the room, 37–39
Fluency, 30
    Building, 16, 61
    Reading, 9
    Writing, 9, 65, 93
From scribbles to competency, 18–19
Frustration zone, 12

Hearing and recording sounds/spelling, 18–19
High expectations for effort/achievement, 20–21

I Kn rit (I can write!), 30, 111
Instruction, 8
    Assumptions about writing, 8
    Explicit, 25
    Extending, 23
    Foundation for writing, 5–30
    One-to-one, 5, 25
    Planning, 22–23
    Timing and content, 18
    Whole-class, 20, 24, 93
    Writing, 6, 8

Kidwriting, 38, 44, 46, 50
    Telling a story with, 51–53
Knowledge of letters, 20

Labeling, 41, 42, 48, 101, 102
    Writing tool for beginners, 40–42
Learning goals, 21
Learning zone, 9, 12
Lists, 74
Literacy-rich environment, 8
Losing unnecessary capital letters, 87

Making a picture that tells a story, 31–33
Making all the sentences belong, 70–72
Making the story make sense to the reader, 106
Mentoring, 5
Monitoring student progress, 33
Morning Message, 25

Narrative, 83, 90, 104
Non-fiction, 100–103, 104
    Adding more information to, 107

Observation, 22–23, 96
Oral language development, 18–19, 23, 35
Oral rehearsal, 16, 35
Oral storytelling, 20, 35, 46
Organizing/organization, 44, 46, 49

Partner talk/work, 16, 32, 33, 35, 39, 58, 68, 72, 78, 81, 90, 93, 94, 102
Phonemics/phonetics, 28–29, 38, 41, 46, 60, 63, 83
Phonics, 28–29
Picture development, 18–19
Picture making, 9, 20, 32, 35, 38, 45, 46–50, 54–56, 102
Poetry, 95–99, 104
    Using poetic devices to improve, 105
Position, 44
Practising capital letters and periods, 86
Pre-writing warm-up, 16
Printing and punctuation, 18–19
Putting more detail in pictures, 54–56

Reading aloud, 15, 16, 25, 55, 58, 65, 71, 74, 80, 90, 96, 101
Reflection, 24–25
Reinforcing the learning
    Making stories from pictures, 46–50
    Reviewing genres, 104–108
    Writing personal stories, 83–88
    Writing stories, 60–63
Remembering details, 73–75
Repetition, 96
Retelling a story, 90, 115
Risk taking, 13
Role playing, 39, 74

Safety, 12–13
Scaffolding, 12
School language, 111
Scribbling, 9, 16, 30
Scribing, 9, 96
Sentence frames, 111
Sentence starters, 38
Shaping a story into a poem, 95–99
Sound-letter matching, 9, 21, 28, 29, 38, 58, 62
Sound-symbol matching, 29, 38, 41, 42, 46, 52, 53
Spelling, 5, 28–29, 38, 60
    Accountability, 29
    Accuracy, 29
    High-frequency words, 83, 85
    Invented, 28, 52
    Phonetic, 60, 83
    Rules, 28–29
Spelling references, 29
Story development/making, 32, 35, 41, 42, 46, 65, 75, 83, 90, 93

Story grammar, 89–91, 104, 116
    Building a story, 92–94
    Map, 90, 114
Story retelling/telling, 34–36, 51–53

Talking out loud, 32, 35, 44
Teachable moments, 11
Teaching
    Explicit, 23–24
    Lessons, 32–33
    Model, 24
Teaching basic tools, 25
Telling a story
    Kidwriting, 51–53
    Picture, 34–36
Thinking through story, 35
Titles, 67–69, 71, 72
Topic choice, 13–15, 65, 68, 83, 104
Transcribing oral stories, 23

Visualizing, 55
Visuals, 111

Webs,
    Non-fiction, 101, 102, 103
    Poetry, 97
    Topic, 66
Word bank, 111
Words
    Copied, 13
    Counting, 52, 53
    Finding more sounds in, 47
    Hearing and recording sounds in, 38
    High-frequency, 29, 83, 85
    Known sight, 13, 38, 52
    Writing, 38
Writer and the writing, 17
Writers
    Beginning, 5, 16, 22
    Confident, 22
    Fluent, 93
    Improving, 16–25
    Knowing, 16–20
    Sitting alongside, 22
    Student, 11–16
    Successful, 12, 60, 83, 88
    Supporting, 12
    Young, 5, 12, 14, 16, 29, 68, 104

Writing
  Act of, 8
  Assumptions about instruction, 8
  Children's, 11, 13
  Climate, 20
  Conventional, 52
  Development, 5, 13, 16, 18–19, 22, 30, 58, 60, 111–112
  Discussion, 15, 38, 55, 57–59, 65, 68, 80, 81, 90, 97, 101
  Effective, 8, 14
  Encouraging, 11–16, 41
  Expectations, 20–21
  Finding time for, 10–11
  Foundation for instruction, 5–30
  Good, 22
  Group, 96
  Improving, 16–25
  Independent, 10, 24
  Interactive, 24, 46
  Kidwriting, 38, 44, 46, 51–53
  Modeling, 32
  Non-fiction, 100–103, 107
  Personal, 65, 66, 68, 74, 83–88, 96
  Poetry, 95–99
  Pretend, 38, 39
  Promoting, 16
  Putting more detail in, 46, 57–59
  Reflection, 24–25
  Rehearsing, 16
  Repetitive, 68
  Spontaneous, 90, 93, 96, 101
  Standard, 52, 53
  Story, 42, 46, 65, 75, 80, 83–88, 90, 93, 94
  Strategies, 11
  Student, 9, 68, 93, 96, 101
  Supporting, 25
  Sustaining attention to, 21
  Sustaining interest in, 10
  Teaching, 5, 6, 9
  Tips for teaching ESL learners about, 113
  Topics for, 14, 15, 22, 65, 68
Writing at the bottom of the page, 43–45
Writing avoidance, 13
Writing dates, 41, 45
Writing development, 5, 13, 16, 18–19
Writing dilemma, 38
Writing dimensions/steps, 52, 83
Writing from your life, 64–66
Writing ideas, 14
Writing Workshop, 5, 10–11, 13, 21, 22, 25, 29, 32, 38, 39, 46, 50, 55, 60, 63, 65, 71, 83, 88, 101, 102, 104, 108, 113
  Beyond, 25–28
  Investing time in, 10–11
  Model for explicit teaching, 24
  Procedures, 13

Zone
  Frustration, 12
  Learning, 9, 12
  Proximal development, 12